THOUGHTS ON MANAGEMENT

THOUGHTS
ON
MANAGEMENT

By

Sashibhusan Rath

Assistant General Manager (HRD)
Rourkela Steel Plant (SAIL)
Rourkela

D P H

DISCOVERY PUBLISHING HOUSE
NEW DELHI-110002

First Published-2005

ISBN 81-8356-007-5

Published by

DISCOVERY PUBLISHING HOUSE
4831/24, Ansari Road, Prahlad Street,
Darya Ganj, New Delhi-110002 (India)
Phone: 23279245 • Fax: 91-11-23253475
E-mail:dphtemp@indiatimes.com

Printed at:

Amit Enterprises, Delhi

Preface

My first book on management was *Essays on Management*. This present volume is a sequel to the earlier one and is an anthology of various articles written by me and published over a decade in journals of repute. My readers have suggested to see all of them in a book form. Hence this book in this shape in your hand.

Books on management are often textual and contain overstretched concepts unless one has sufficient time in hand reading becomes tedious. Here I have tried to be lucid and in the course of that certain generalistic statements might have unintentionally crept in for which I may be excused. This book has small essays touching Kutilya, HRD, Trade Union, PR, Environment, Safety etc. At the end there are words, aphorisms.

I am grateful to my colleagues, peers, superiors, subordinates in my work-life and to innumerable people whom I observed over a long period of time as they were the stuff of food for the mind. My thanks to my wife Sanghamitra, sons Ritayan and Rishikesh who never disliked my brooding time. Mr. Tilak Wasan deserves a special word of thanks for taking up its publication quickly.

This book is humbly dedicated to my parents Sri Chandrasekhar Rath and Smt. Charubala Rath who have been sacrificing so much for me till date.

My efforts will be amply rewarded if the readers get something substantial from this book.

—Author

Preface

Contents

1

A Vision of Human Resource in IT Millennium

IT: Hallmark of the Millennium

Winston Churchill had curtly said the empires of the future would be the empires of the mind. Alvin Toffler too says that the economics of the world have evolved in three stages: agricultural, industrial and post-industrial and the post industrial has been named as the 'information age' by Bill Gate and this new millennium has ushered into what we call the IT Millennium. Millennium ago, advanced technology consisted of farming and irrigation, today we talk of global optical fiber networks. Progress with a mind of its own, rules inexorably downstream, each swell of advancement changing the course of the river—but at an invisible pace. We are not at the dawn of a new age, we are in the stream already.

Advancement of IT has become the sine qua non of economic development in the modern world. It is not easy to insulate any country from IT invasion. The three main forces which are the main drivers of reshaping the present in the new millennium are: info-tech, globalisation and awakening the mankind. Faster reflexes, quicker decision making are the in-thing. The expectation of a profound revolution is in-built in human consciousness and is arising out of this digital era. Infotech and awakening of humans shall revolutionise the organisation into a flexible and dynamic entity with networks of empowered and intelligent workers.

In the IT age intellectual capital has become the key word—it is knowledge that is of value to an organisation. Its main elements are human capital, structural capital and customer capital. IT has therefore, by design developed the capability to untangle the knots of our knowledge by creating this facility of a substitute cognitive response apparatus. IT has started making jobs more enjoyable and existing human resource (HR) is becoming more conscious of the business ethics, its social and ecological aspects. Successful marriage of the controlled people and a benevolent organisation can only create wealth. The characteristics of present time is unfamiliarity, uncertainty and unpredictability but still everyday there is electronic marketing of one trillion dollars. Global village has become a reality. Companies have also started ensuring more meaning to work-life and private life.

Knowledge Society

We are already in a knowledge society. There is subtle difference between information and knowledge. Information means data arranged in meaningful pattern and knowledge means something that is believed, that is true and reliable. It is easy to transfer information from one place to another but very difficult to transfer knowledge from one person to another. Knowledge is not as tangible as information. Aptly said T.S. Eliot (British poet, 1888-1967):

"Where is the knowledge which is lost in information?

And where is the wisdom that is lost in knowledge?"

Business processes will be redefined around knowledge. Informed knowledge workers will flock those organisations which give more compensation package and higher satisfaction. Leaders have now started discovering that meaning an organisation means managing a knowledge society and he has to be a knowledge leader or chief knowledge officer (CKO). The world talks about knowledge today which is Indian culture for the last thousands of years!

Knowledge Management (KM) means lot more than just coping with IT enabled organisational and strategic architectures. Fundamentally it translates itself into a formidable task of realigning the new possibilities arising out of IT with the basic dynamics of knowledge creation and development. K.M delivers the intellectual capacity of the firms to the knowledge workers who guide to the success or failure of a business. As such information processing capability will be the source of competitive advantage. Information can be sold or bought easily, therefore management of knowledge will have the leverage. KM is based on the power of learning that never gets obsolete. In thinking organisation all the three times viz. past, present and future will be understood, assessed and strategised.

The proper management clearly lies along a complex balanced middle path, acquiring constant judgement and continuing adjustment. Such equilibrium thinking guides emotions and thoughts, two major driving forces of humanity. Equilibrium is higher order of stability than balance. Equilibrium is balance in motion and calls for creative responses to the demands of the moment.

Therefore whatever may be the business the name of the game is business.

Changing Concept of Organisation

No enterprise can be guided into future without clear understanding of the commercial, political and social impact of global economy. We see that the walls between markets, organisations and customers are crumbling; corporations and customers are moving freely in and out of their countries, 21st century organisations will be necessarily flat, networked and amorphous. There is transition from 20th century value chains to the anarchic networks of the new millennium. Net has started influencing business radically:

- Clearing memory and unlearning have become all the more necessary;
- Any mismatch between training and actual work is not cost-effective;

- Competition no longer is for capital or technology but for the people;
- Corporate battles are won by well-informed superior human capital;
- Systems have become more inclusive rather than more exclusive.

Business, Technology and Strategy are the three fundamental elements whose synergy decide the success and failure of any industrial organisation. The 4Es of winning edge are: Economy, Efficiency, Effectiveness and Excellence. KM or Knowledge Management as mentioned earlier is the antidote to the failing situation.

Vast equipment proliferation, lack of professionals are soon leading to out-sourcing. Most of the activities will be out-sourced. By out-sourcing to the third party the other two get the professionalism. Two hundred years ago, Adam Smith had rightly written, " the maxim of every prudent master is never to attempt to make at home, what it will cost him more to make than to buy". In this millennium a number of services and functions are being out-sourced. In the last three decades companies have been outsourcing only peripheral services in the last three decades like cleaning, security etc. but now it is the turn around in the core functions and services. It is crucial to define what is core and what is peripheral. Core is being rigidly, controlled and protected to withstand long term competition.

Due to changing business philosophy of more sophisticated information system, departments' outsourcing have now grown to span multiple systems like transfer of assets, lease and staff to a vendor who assumes the total profit and loss responsibility. Vendors actually operate, manage and control the IT function and the organisation remains only titular.

Global competitive pressure, continuous technological innovations, concurrent socio-economic changes are forcing organisations globally to rethink the manner in which they transact business and wherever necessary re-engineer themselves. "Do more with less" is the demand of the time. "To do things differently" is the solution to this demand. Information Communication Technology System is a powerful tool to operate and achieve in the changing organisations. The finite elements of competitive edge the present organisations are:

— Reviewing design/systems parameters with a view to achieving targeted cost;

— Better management of working capital;

— Coordinated sourcing;

— Better utilisation and sharing fixed cost across divisions;

— Meeting international specifications e.g. quality, time, service etc.;

— Forming synergetic portfolios and networking;

— Clearly spelling out ARA (authority, responsibility and accountability);

— Vibrant human relationship;

— Repetitive documents can be curtailed through computerisation;

— Moving to smaller and compact premises may be distant but IT connected;

— To offer better value to customers in the most cost-effective way rather than the competition.

World Economy, Human Capital and IT

World economy has transformed from a production based value to a knowledge based value. What we call the global economy is really the conjunction of five forces:

- *Booming Spot Economies:* Hong Kong, Taiwan, Bangalore has little dependence on their respective central governments. Solid line national border is becoming dotted line between nations resulting in migration of capital, information, products and services. Traditional role of protectionism is changing.

- *Cultural Revolution by Media:* Emergence of global class of young consumers. Nike, Sony, Toyota, Motorola, Coca Cola are familiar names everywhere due to media projection.
- *Cost Sharing Through Revenue Saturation:* In order to minimise cost and to maximise revenue, a method of saturating the appetite of the consumers can be developed.
- *Emergence of New Leaders:* Leaders are growing to be strategic leaders, they have understood how to build networks rather than pyramids. Instead of directing the work of others they have started to learn sharing, sorting and synthesising information.
- *Energetic youth:* The young generation dominating the IT industry has refuted most of the well established theories of recruitment, motivation, training etc.

Economics of scale and capital merely provide a foothold but not the competitive edge. It is done through effective use of the abilities of people through acquiring, creating and using knowledge for increasing higher value addition for all. Other alternative is an outsourcing contract: outsourcing company and the contractor. Besides these two there is an equally significant party which is equally affected by the company's outsourcing contract—it is the employees. Therefore employer must also think about the future of the existing HR i.e. the employee. Employer has to think of either of the standard social security system viz. alternative job or severance compensation. Transfer of employees to vendors have resulted into labour problems and after lengthy negotiation and litigations with employees suitable compensation is decided and paid. Employees are legally, economically and socially affected by the change of employer as a result of outsourcing.

India enjoys a substantial competitive advantage in the global economy by virtue of its knowledge resources in science, technology and engineering coupled with a large base of skilled English speaking manpower. Knowledge is the new basis for wealth. How one controls or owns knowledge is in fact a central issue in a knowledge based economy. All are now knowledge workers. India has manpower of high calibre. The software industry in India today is valued at Rs. 63.1 billion and employs nearly 1.6 lakh people. By 2005 it is expected to be 50 billion US dollars and 22 lakh respectively. It must not head towards the abyss of mediocrity. India need not recycle knowledge for the west, it has her own indigenous ideas. At different levels evolution is happening:

- **International**
  - world is becoming a global village;
  - international collaboration, inter-dependency;
  - networking.
- **National**
  - awareness of literacy and quality;
  - citizens are becoming customers;
  - wired society.
- **Local**
  - virtual office/corporation;
  - flexibility and adaptability;
  - equal and instant access.

Similarly in the economic and technological fronts also there are changes:

- **Economic**
  - cost counter approach;
  - professionalism and managerialism;
  - value for money;
  - LPG (liberalisation, privatisation and globalisation);
  - tele-economy.
- **Technological**
  - emergence of telematics;

- convergence of computers and telecommunications;
- OFT (optical fiber technology) digital revolution;
- information super highways.

But to stay ahead of this emerging global competition and knowledge leverage, five critical areas require immediate attention: education and training, research, communication, intellectual property rights and human resource management.

All are equally important but the HRM challenge is: to create a conducive climate in India, to attract and retain talent in a borderless and globalised environment. Talent is now footloose and seeks out the best opportunity, quality of life world wide. Everyone knows that only great people—not just great processes nor systems of financial power are essential for a company to succeed.

Organisation now is essentially an information processing system. IT has the potential of the social transformation. We are rapidly moving into a future of which we know little. Our statistical and forecasting methods are inadequate to gauge the future. Therefore:

- we can hardly afford to function in the old style, hierarchical structure and bureaucratic culture of rule obsession culture;
- unnecessary moral codes will be curtailed and there will be unfettered free space;
- there will be transparency and free flow of information;
- there will be better control and good management;
- managers will decide what information is necessary or not for running their organisation;
- systems become more inclusive rather than exclusive;
- computers are capturing control over many perceptual layers of knowledge;
- through pervasive computing pushes ahead, computers seem destined to enter the conceptual and individual domains of knowledge as well;

- computers make us free to take on newer tasks and greater creative challenges.

There is no escape from IT impact, multimedia, e-commerce, artificial intelligence, virtual reality network simulation are the most intrusive technology wares in human history. In every era there have been people who recognised forces that would change everything. And there have been people who could not see what was in front of them. The former prospers and the latter perishes. Those who do not respond to change soon become extinct like the dinosaur. It is true for business organisation as well as living organisms. Upgrading quality of people using communication and technology appropriately like through information networking, telecommunication, teleconferencing, video-conferencing etc. this liability can be transformed into an asset.

HR manager is to listen with his people really want from the organisation. If the employees lower level needs remain unaddressed everything you do for them further along the journey is almost irrelevant. On the other hand if these needs are successfully met the team building and innovating becomes much easier. Great managers must hold a minor to the employees and encourage them to look into the mirror—to know themselves better and to know the roles they perform.

Then he tells the management to meet such requirements by translating the deepest wants. A great work place is to be created where best people would love to stay and work. Conventional systems will be required to be uprooted ruthlessly by the HR anarchists. Focus is on improving capability of the workforce. There has to be evolutionary improvement path from ad hoc, inconsistently performing workforce practices to a mature, disciplined development of workforce. Attracting quality manpower, retaining them and improving their skills is a critical component of any company. High attrition rate can be brought down by addressing people-oriented issues which serves the purpose of retaining manpower. It is time to modify the HR strategies to manage the HR of the millennium. HR systems need to be redefined and restructured because the new generation workforce is: innovative, risk-taking and adaptive. Chairman of Infosys has rightly said, "My assets walk out of the gate every night".

HR in organisations are to be geared up to improve the bottom line on a sustained basis. There is a need to break free from conventional box and pull up the socks to stay ahead in the rat race and also to be in the IT invasion. No body would like to cut off a limb but if gangrene sets in one has to take harsh decision however painful it may be. Same is the case of wedding out human resources which are no longer required. With a view to optimising manpower every individual is to be a quality and customer oriented.

Leaders to invest personally in the process of developing future leaders, thereby building the most precious organisational assets. The success of leaders cannot be measured by whether they win today or tomorrow but whether the company is winning in the next 10/15 years hence when the new generation of leaders take over. Leadership is no longer commandership—it is managing the future.

Human beings are social animals, and work is a social institution. Acceptance, appreciation and affection are the three A's which make a better environment. Allow friendship to flower at work place. Treating people as equal, fixing workers weaknesses, training people for skills they do not have etc. all these will be antiquated. Even rules are becoming extinct. The innate yearning to learn and grow is natural to human beings. To learn is to grow in today's continuously changing and competitive environment. Ceteris paribus, no organisation is valued more by people than the one that enables them to learn.

The human factor in enterprises play an important role in management field. Individuals are much more than merely productive factor in the management plan. Power of the people is indomitable. Knowledge is the new ware. People are the new power. Constructing human network and information network helps in catching human nerve.

Human capital is knowledge, skill and competencies of the people in an organisation. Structural capital consists of structures, process, information system, patents etc. which remain even after employees leave. Customer capital is the value of organisational relationship with its customers. Quality to be harnessed. To be innovative, disciplined home work before launching anything new is necessary.

Mind is dominating over matter. Human life is now more precious than it was before. There will be no war across the borders but in air-conditioned rooms between the personal computers and these energetic, impatient youth is the major issue for the HR specialist in this new millennium. They are adaptable, creative, enterprising but govt. jobs and pensions do not attract them. What they want is a balanced employer-employee relationship. They want flexitime or flexibility. They enjoy dead line—give them clear direction, resources, parameters, guidelines and counselling, if required and also:

— Be patient with their mistakes and risk-taking habits;

— Do not try to suppress creative instrincts;

— Combine responsibility with authority;

— Treat difficulties as opportunities for learning;

— People like to be on the move;

— More accessibility is also liked.

Youth's aspirations need not stop at being personal rather they are to be more social and national.

Most of the Indian intellectuals have accepted to play subordinate role. They are subordinate to those in power so that they can share it or to those who are abroad so that they can make money and bask in the reflected glory. When will our own ideas begin to matter to us?

Can creativity be copied? A contradiction in terms. Creativity still blooms in India as a result of individual efforts and not what the system brings forth: Vicious cycle of mediocrity and indifference is to be thwarted.

Postcript

Job evolved in response to basic shift called industrialisation. It is time for another shift. Automation, outsourcing, mass production, privatisation of public services—all mean that the circumstances which made the job necessary and now disappearing or changing. Death of job is inevitable. Therefore it is judicious not to resist a change that has already happened, but find ways to work with that change. Society has started recognising itself with the job-shift. Very soon no one will have a job. Job is a social artifact. It is so deeply embedded in our consciousness that most of us have forgotten its artificiality and the fact that since the beginning of time societies have thrived without jobs.

Society has started recognising itself with the job-shift. Very soon no one will have a job. Job is a social artifact. It is so deeply embedded in our consciousness that most of us have forgotten its artificiality and the fact that since the beginning of time societies have thrived without jobs. Society may return to a more natural way of working with assignments or projects in various fields, broken by periods of rest or inactivity. Individuals will be adequately paid for time spent in the economic activity of society and they will also engross in self-chosen activities which will provide self-fulfillment.

Psychological implications of dejobbing will occur. Job has becomes the focus of many peoples' lives, it structures peoples' time and provide order and stability. For many people the jobs define who they are not just what they do. All these will be lost. There will be many temporary workers not employed in conventional sense. Conventional avenues of employment shall disappear opening up avenues for new ones.

In Information society industry will continue to flourish, but its products will be provided by the much smaller proportion of workforce than in the hey day of industrial era. No country will be able to ignore the onslaught of IT or slow down its actualisation. There may be acquisition of high degree of power—but how to prohibit the consolidation of such power in the hands of unscrupluous leaders will be a challenge. There will be sharp distinction between the 'minority who know' and the 'majority who do not know'. The deeper psychological and sociological consequences of information society and still more difficult to discuss at this stage today.

Poised on the brink of a social revolution ushered by modern IT the world has two choices:

- to continue pursuing material goals and selfish aims and thereby cause the slow but sure decline of all world systems;
- to unite and work towards building an improved life for future generation.

In this context Adi Shankaracharya, the 8th century Indian philosopher saint said: "Time flies, our lives run out, and yet we are unable to overcome our insatiable urge for acquiring more and more worldly possessions". This reiterated by contemporary French philosopher Gaston Berger, "We must no longer wait for tomorrow, it has to be invented".

Knowledge and social relations are becoming complex with three afflictions: plethora of knowledge, anachronism and unsuitability. What is necessary is acquiring and developing, critical faculties, awareness of self-knowledge , overcoming undesirable destructive behaviour, enabling global view, permanently activating creative or imaginative faculties etc.

Jack Welch said, 'Control your destiny or some one else will'.

2

Strategies for Human Resources

A Vision of 21st Century

The world is in a state of flux. Rapid strides are being made in most areas of human behaviour. We are poised to witness a far greater mobility of capital and labour. Distances are shrinking. In this era of liberalisation and globalisation a manager can hardly function effectively unless he continuously updates his knowledge and homes his skills; he is also required to keep his eyes and ears open to the happenings within the firm he works and the experiences of the related systems/firm.

We are moving:

From: Monolithic, vertical, homogeneous, unit, medium pace etc.

To: divergent, horizontal, centralised, heterogenous, flat, network, fast pace etc.

We have all started living in an unpatient world with fierce competition and fleeting opportunities. Profile of today's situation is:

- The world around is cruel;
- One's ally of yesterday is a competitor today;

- Customers demand value for money;
- Employee's loyalty is a thing of the past;
- In changing times rules have to be continually rewritten;
- It does not take long for skill and knowledge to get outdated;
- Technological advance and the flood of new information often makes it difficult to keep up.

One is required to move faster, better with less time and money. Customers centricity will be the organisational focus. Very soon the productivity of knowledge and knowledge workers will not be the only competitive factor but also the decisive factor for rise or fall of business organisation. Traditional information (which is 90 per cent of total information) related to what goes on inside an organisation will be fast replaced by new power pointed information. A winning strategy will require information about events, conditions, resources, etc. outside organisation like non-customers, markets not served presently, parallel technologies, present competitors, human resources and their skill of competing organisation etc.

Learning to Strategise

Sun Tzu, a native of Wu province was an ancient Chinese strategist. His two dictums are still valid for any business organisation:

Dictum-1: The way to certain victory is to always have unfathomable wisdom and an unfailing way.

Dictum-2: Those who triumph a hundred times against a hundred conflicts don't have supreme skill. Those who have supreme skill use strategy to bend others without coming to conflict.

Preparatory measures for formalising any strategy:

- To analyse the situation, a large number of factors must be delved into before meeting any challengel;
- To gather any kind of information. Inadequacy of information has elements of failure;

- Pre-action and post-action impact on economy to be assessed;
- To access the other end also to assess oneself from strength and weakness point of view;
- To position tactically so that triumph is effortless and destructive conflict is averted;
- Slated blue-print must be practical and implementable.

The premise of strategy is that human being is a scarce organisational resource. "People" is the key word. The human factor is an integral part of corporate strategy. Intensely competitive business, technological transformation, information revolution etc., and their impact on industry and organisation is to be accessed while making a strategy.

What share of future opportunities can we capture with our current portfolio of core competencies is the key question. And we have to identify and maximise those core competencies to have the future opportunities in our favour. In a competitive field effective strategy formulation is of crucial significance. To strategise effectively one has to examine one's strengths, weaknesses, opportunities and threats (SWOT). These are the means. These are easier said than done.

Learning to adopt a new paradigm at right tune is also relevant to this context. Paradigm is a set of rules and regulations which establish boundaries, telling you how to work within them and help measure your success as the ability to solve problems within those paradigm. Paradism has a life of its own. In the first phase when you are figuring out what rules are applicable, there is a plateau. Then comes the growth phase where the paradigm is being used to easily solve problems. The final stage shows the slowing down when the more difficult problems are being tackled and the success rate is still slower. By which it is the right time to adopt a new paradigm.

Human Capital: The People

A company is not built out of money only but out of people, processors and systems. For reinventing and organisation we have got to assert human capital: people as its most important strategic resource. Human beings can make or break an organisation.

Technology is not nature, but man. It is not about tools only; it is about how man works. It is equally about how man lives and how man thinks. There is a saying of Alfred Russell Wallace (1823-1913), the co-discover with Charles Darwin of the Theory of Evolution: "Man is the only animal capable of being directed for purposeful evolution; he makes tools". Since technology is an extension of man, basic technological change expresses our world view and in turn, changes it.

Goethe's wisdom is strategic and relevant to HR: Treat a man as he is, and he will remain as he is; treat a man as he can and should be, and he will become as he can and should be". Therefore, one is to believe in the unseen human potential otherwise there will be only status quo in the business performance; and that is not going to cut a mark. Long term investment for improving quality of human capital is a very important element in our competitiveness.

HR—Strategy

Business enterprise at their inception are primarily economic entities but as they grow the emphasis shifts towards a more social character. Its actionsare to be justifiable in terms of spirit in which society allows it to function. Organisation are also cradles of power games and political behaviour hence cannot be totally divorced from political governance.

Unless the political culture of organisation change, responsible corporate governance will remain true in alphabets only. Corporate governance is not blind adherence to externally imposed norms and codes only but a commitment to the spirit of internally developed management ethos.

Management is not a mere discipline but a culture with its own values, beliefs, tools. In today's complex environment a manager can hardly thrive on native brilliance and intuitive understanding of the situation he confronts. Management is interdisciplinary by nature: an engineer manager knowing only engineering is not enough, he has to have understanding of the social, political, legal and economic environment within which he has to operate. He is also required to know behavioural science, information technology, the way finances is managed, the way the structures and systems operate within the firm, the strategic implication of his actions and inactions and so on and so forth. To groom managers to be fit to survive is necessary.

The impacts of technology are actually more difficult to predict than most other developments. Economic and social prophets have the dismal record as predictors of technology and its impacts. There once the technology becomes effective careful monitoring of the actual impact (both beneficial and detrimental) is essential. Monitoring is a managerial responsibility and requires to be exercised.

Challenges from external environment are such that only conventional, wisdom cannot suffice, managing requires creative solutions to problems. Passing the blame, criticising the system will not do.

One has to be sensitive to various issues:

— To be multifunctional;

— To be multidisciplinary;

— To be multisector think-tank;

— To disperse rapidly new knowledge;

— To disperse rapidly new capibilities;

— To have distilled knowledge reservoir about place and people.

In the coming age of new technology worker and work cannot be organised if planning is divorced from doing. More planning a worker does and the more responsibilities he takes for what he does, the more productive he can be. A worker who does only as instructed can do only harm.

People need roots. One needs a management structure which magnifies and indeed respects the roots of a person and yet a true team with diversities is made.

Binding between employer and worker can be achieved either through life-time employment (as is in Japan) or through partnership in times of profit and loss.

Predictability of behaviour and action is required. Rules and laws help make behaviour predictable but total adherance is not a good way to assure success. Farming of rules must include organisational culture.

Redundancy may be in the skills of workmen and also in the total learning available with managers. If redundancy is present the CEO is to leave his cocoon of "Deciding and Directing" to "Managing Organisational Learning". Top team must examine and improve its own ability to learn.

People today don't want to be "used" by the organisation as "Victims" or "Pawn". Rather they want:

- To have a stewardship on whatever resources they own;
- To feel that they are making a personal contribution to something meaningful;
- The organisation should empower them to take decisions;
- The organisation encouraging them to develop a feeling of ownership;
- An atmosphere of learning and development exists.

"Meltingpot" assimilation of culture is out; "Salad bowl" concept is in. Culturally diverse workers want to be "themselves" and retain their cultural identities. They resist conforming to the "one size fits all" organisational culture. Politically correctness may sometimes make a mockery of the human resource.

Empowerment is the in thing. It involves trust and demands true leadership. Effective delegation no longer means delegation only but release of authority as well as giving of responsibility.

Hierarchies are replaced by self-managing structures like networks, multidisciplinary teams etc. If not done to do it in order to match with develcpments.

Time has came to came to choose from opacity and transparency. Opacity (opaqueness) means plethora of complex rules, compartmentalisation, information limited to very few. Transparency means established simple norms, massive flow of information across the interfaces. Transparency returns good dividends.

Integrating Human Resource Management (HRM) to Corporate Strategy (CS) poses two ways:

1. Breakdown Maintenance Strategy (BMS)
2. Preventive Maintenance Strategy (PMS)

BMS is followed by Indian companies under circumstances when management fall out with trade unions and adopt the ABCD formula (Agitation, Bargain, Confrontation and Demand) since the ABCD are directly linked with Indian labour legislation. Whenever there is a dispute; weak decision, only short term solutions, divide and rule methods transpire. Some progressive companies, however, follow PMS by encouraging group activities. Management union relationship is safeguarded. Adequate care is taken before any relational rupture.

Broadly speaking the overall profile of business scenario is as follows (which are also some kind of factors to strategise):

- In family enterprise top post is inherited;
- In private sector centralised control;
- In private sector a closed system, divide and rule policy;
- In public sector top heavy administration;
- In public sector limited tenure of chief executives;
- In public sector multilevel and slow decision making process;
- In multinational a highly specialised management;
- In multinational a high turnover;
- In multinational stiff competition, deadline;
- In multinational frequent mergers, trimming of staffs etc.

In view of all these integrating the two HRM strategies i.e. BMS and PMS with the corporate strategy (CS) is a challenging job. For linking certain steps can be taken:

Core Level

1. Be proactive instead of reactive;
2. Integral management approach contrary to fire fighting;
3. To grow core areas.

Structural Level

4. Destaffing, staffing and restaffing wherever required only for business strategy point of view;
5. Matrix of responsibility, authority, accountability;
6. Team of self propelled managers (not those "look busy", "pensioner" type);
7. Scientific monitoring.

Implementation Level

8. To change mind-set;
9. Awareness of objective and compare data at all levels;
10. Clarity of customers, what they want for others;
11. Ensuring shop floor employees capable of implementing top decision.

Epilogue

It is not enough to imagine the future, you also have to build it, sometimes blue-print is available, foresight is there but there is no capacity to execute. In corporate sense a strategic architecture is the link between the present and the future.

Goal cannot be achieved by linear thinkers. Learn the linear way, but then unlearn and create. Go beyond strategic planning to "strategic thinking" as a continuum to succeed. Peter Senge says in the Fifth Discipline that learning to see underlying structures rather than events is of importance.

Can't an organisation have a CBP (Code of Best Practice) to cherish in addition to the usual routine Personnel Manual or Establishment Manual!

The activities which are the "conscience" of an oganisation must never be subordinated to anything else not it should be placed with any other activity, it should rather be clearly separate. These are "giving vision", "setting standards", "quantum of change and change analysis" etc. Conscience work is incompatible with "operating" or "giving advice". The organisation to be made to accept the competence and integrity of such conscience executive. Enthusiasm is at the bottom of progress. With it, there is accomplishment; without it, there are only alibis.

3

Re-engineering

The Concept

The term Re-engineering was first introduced in the common business usage in 1990 in a seminal Harvard Business Review article authored by Michel Hammar. The original concept since then has been in use as well as in misuse by managers and consultants across the world. It is the most popular management concept today both in developed as well as developing nations.

The terms in use can be defined as:

Engineering: Value is added to the technique by combination of a few elements.

Re-engineering: Value is added to the technique by re-arranging a few elements.

Business Process Re-engineering (BPR): Adding value by re-arranging the business process.

Re-engineering promises dramatic improvements in performance. The underlying idea is of fundamental rethinking and radical redesign of business process rather than tinkering with the activities/tasks within the functional and skill-based groupings in the organisation. Re-engineering has a simplicity of its own which aims at delivering value to the customer. It can be treated as a wonder-drug for the Indian corporate structures, also as a curative for the weak and the ailing and also as a tonic for healthy organisations which race for survival and want to go ahead of others!

As a general drug re-engineering cannot be administered to any kind of organisation. It entails a fundamentals breakthrough in mindset i.e. challenging the past wisdom, well accepted values and methods of doing things etc. Breaking the standard framework of the enterprise wherever required is a normal re-engineering effort.

For any re-engineering efforts to succeed it needs a leader at the top who should be daring with a passionate desire to change and create a new customer focused organisational activities. Such a top management should also be able to define bold aspirations, take difficult and sometimes even unpopular decisions without affecting the enthusiasm across the hierarchy.

Re-engineering efforts, will therefore be a painful exercise for those organisations which lack committed leadership, strategic focus ambitious and practicable goals. For such organisations quick, dramatic improvements remain a far cry. Choosing the 'right scale' and 'spot' of re-engineering efforts within the company is the key to harvesting the gains with manageable risk.

Empowerment is complementary to re-engineering and it focuses strongly on developing people's skill and potential. It is a shift in philosophy; which questions all the old relationships and assumptions. If influences the way work is done as well as how people relate to each other. Irrespective of the position everyone has something to gain from empowerment. Everyone is a leader and traditional leader don't always exercise that role of empowerment. Unless empowerment approach is used by manufacturing and service industries they will cease to the successful in the increasingly competitive and rapidly changing world. Carry out bold power transfer.

Re-engineering and HR

In a re-engineered organisation, employees usually gain greater prestige and importance. When the re-engineered process gives a critical competitive edge to the company, those who are a part of that process become much more important to the company.

Re-engineering after all is not about down-sizing. It is also not about restructuring. It changes the organisation of the work itself it will be incorrect to say re-engineering will never result in the loss of jobs. Useless or wasteful work to be removed completely. Abolishing of jobs which have been considered obvious so far. Some jobs infact may be merged into one position, others may be eliminated. Such displaced worker may move from 'old position' to 'more important jobs' newly created by re-engineering.

HR professionals are to be aware of the need and difficulty in moving the executives through 3 phases of their developments:

(i) Discipline expert;

(ii) Functional manager;

(iii) Business manager.

Similarly in Business Process Engineering (BPE) employees are invited to experience 3-things:

(i) Become aware of business realties, going beyond functional, discipline loyalties;

(ii) Develop process sensitivity, as distinct from a pre-occupation with activities;

(iii) Proactive design of the methods, systems and procedures, rather than reactively let things happen.

Re-engineering is also a part of pursuit of excellence in the areas of marketing, products and cost management and the path of excellence is shown below:

Marketing: From routine reply of complaints
to
customer satisfaction
onto
customer delight

Products: From traditional routine products
to
successive generation of new products.

Cost: From cost information
Management: to
cost control based on standards
onto
cost reduction challenging the standards
themselves.

In the flow of any company's life one needs to carry people and to engage in BPR1, BPR2, ...BPRn.

Modern management tools like TQM, bench-marking, Kaizan, Delayering etc. 'attempt to change the business' from the way it is carried out now. Re-engineering calls for the recognising from the very scratch of the structures, systems and procedures, products and processes. Re-engineering is easier to say but difficult to do without strong commitment by the top management.

HR professional's activities will no longer be limited to HRD instruments only but his job will involve evolution of an 'all encompassing vision' involving all levels of men. Peter Senge in The Fifth Discipline says "Don't push growth, remove the factors limiting the growth".

A few innovative measures like the following may also be required by some organisations to be taken up soon:

(i) Attractive packages on incentives, gift education;

(ii) Consultants becoming executives and vice versa;

(iii) Blurred boundaries of management between executive and staff;

(iv) Introduction of flexi-time, instead of routine;

(v) Specialisation will introduce, knowledge workers' than workers;

(vi) Shortening of cycle time through concurrent processing.

The expectations from HR professionals are to keep their minds open, keep on learning while updating to comprehend and act upon 'here and now'.

Employee Self-renewal

Just be applying techniques like re-engineering will not yield high performance. The absorption of hard or soft technologies depend on the willingness and competency of individual employees. Therefore, exposure of all employees to 6-dimensional model of personal growth is required:

- Spiritual;
- Aesthetic;
- Intellectual;
- Psychological;
- Material;
- Physical.

Raising spiritual appreciation of their role to organisation as well as society and future generation; bringing them a sense of aesthetic beauty to appreciate newness, new technologies, processes, packaging etc., giving them physical and mental hygiene by extending model medical methods, services and inspiring that personal prosperity follows high level of performance of organisation they serve are necessary for self-renewal of employees. Elucidating the meaning further we have to open new vistas of work-life keeping in view the following:

(i) *Spiritual Awareness:* Western behavioural scientists give more emphasis on employees 'soul' going far beyond 'head' and 'heart';

(ii) *Aesthetic Taste:* Quality of worklife and more so life itself is enriched by a taste for beauty. Kala (art) strengthens kaushalam (skill);

(iii) *Intellectual Depth:* Read and expose oneself to data within one's own organisation and other related industries as well. Knowledge improves action;

(iv) *Psychological Sensitivity:* Nurture friendliness (maitri) and compassion (karuna).

(*v*) *Material Prosperity:* Four legitimate life goals are viz. kama (desire), artha (wealth), dharma (righteosness), moksha (transcendence). If we create and model core values employees will surely seek methods like BPR to deliver results and earn rewards;

(*vi*) *Physical Fitness:* Self alienation is bad. A healthy body can perform goodwork.

Today's Situation

As firms grew and technology became more complicated, it was impossible to carry for any one person, the entire knowledge load. Specialists and managers were hired and formed into the characteristics compartments and echelons of bureaucracy. The knowledge load had to be diffused throughout the managerial ranks.

Today a parallel process is at work. Just as owners became dependent on managers for knowledge; managers too are becoming dependent on their employees for knowledge. Information therefore can be made common property. Constructing information network and human network helps in catching human nerve.

The old smoke-stack division of the firm into "heads" and "hands" no longer works. The separation of "thinking" and "doing" in the traditional model is hardly in keeping with rapid technological progress. Because technologies are more complicated and turnover more frequent than in the past, workers are expected to learn more about adjacent and successive jobs.

In some firms today workers choose the kind of sand papers, switch on and off lighting at their work places. They learn how the plant runs and how customers respond to their work. Many companies have to unlearn a lot of their past and also to forget it. It is because that the future need not be an extrapolation of the past.

For escaping the gravitational pull of the past one should be willing challenge one's own orthodoxies, to regenerate one's own core strategies and rethink about one's fundamental assumptions about how one is going to compete. To shoot into future is almost like a space rocket—portions of which don't contain any fuel for journey are to be jettisoned i.e. relieving the burden of the past. Senior managers feel for it as they had contributed for building the past which now is an excess baggage to be discarded!

If the organisation suffers from. "This is not my responsibility' syndrome one remembers Pat Mitchell who writes in The Kingdom was Lost for lack of 3A:

Attitude: Few people will deny responsibility for performance, but one needs the correct mental attitude to make it happen;

Awareness: We must be clear about the particular contribution we can make. We must recognise our strengths and weaknesses; find ways to build the former and compensate the later;

Action: Responsibility is just a word. Unless it spurs us to action it is of little use.

In a world of professional work, key to personal success is to become a professional. It doesn't mean everyone to have degrees/ diplomas but it means that we have to transform ourselves into the kind of people who fill up professional posts. Some professions require 'process-centred' as well as 'service-centred' roles. Process-centred man must become an operations professional, knowledgeable about manufacturing or production process and how to make it work. Similarly, service-centred man is required to be a professional problem-solver, not merely answering predictable set of customer inquiries but visualising problem areas for taking proactive actions. Everyone must have a professional mind-set.

Success in any profession has three prerequisites: Knowledge, Perspective and Attitude. No professional can succeed without solid grounding in basic discipline which he requires to apply and the knowledge of a professional goes for beyond the basic skill. Personal commitment to learning the particular skill required by the job, a professional must know the concepts of the field, the principles and ideas that have longer lifetimes and those facts and techniques which are changing.

In major re-engineering efforts the reason of failure arises out of inability to mobilise the company's workforce to buy into change. The natural tendency of the people to resist change however continuous to persist.

4

Re-engineering the Human Capital

The Root is Man

The root is man. The goal too is man. Man is not a mass of flesh, bones, blood-water conglomeration only. With this turn of the millennium we have to have a management with a difference. Unless the dignity of man is recognised he will be reduced to a personnel with a staff number only, a commodity who will be kept motivate through payment, incentive etc., at once unserviceable he will be discarded. But is it right? Should technology shrink the conscience of man at the cost of bloating his ego?

Man needs to take a pause from breathless pursuit and see where he is actually heading to. Machines and computers never make a business successful—it is the people. Technology makes things possible but it is the people who make it happen. Human beings occupy a central place in this knowledge and information era. The slogan these days is 'Either Evolve or Dissolve, Choice is Yours'.

Changing Times

This is a period of profound social, economic and political change. Considering rapid obsolescence in different areas people need to be prepared to take up m ore than one career. An antiquated structure and a leisurely procedure are incompatible with the fulfillment of demands of the future. Human obsolescence needs as much attention as technological obsolescence. Ralph Waldo Emerson had rightly said, 'People see only what they are prepared to see.

Micro-level adjustment calls for reorientation of work, values, organisational beliefs, structures etc. But strategies, structures, systems etc. will be soon replaced by purpose, process and people. New breeds of knowledge workers will emerge. Only 'left brain' style of logical and analytical approach will not do and one has to blend analysis with insights. Power and wealth will now rest on knowledge and information. There will be a shift from 'position power' to 'relationship power'. Redundancy of labour and their utilisation through redeployment and knowledge upgradation will be crucial to industry. As strikes are becoming more and more unsuccessful there will be need for co-operation not conflict.

Re-engineering

Engineering (E), Re-engineering (RE) and Business Process Re-engineering (BPR) can be explained as:

E: Method which combines a few elements of science to obtain value;

RE: Method of re-arranging a few elements to add more value;

BPR: Method of internationally rearranging the business process for getting enhanced value.

Re-engineering looks at the way work is done as well as how people relate to each other. It empowers people. Empowerment is complementary to re-engineering. Re-engineering is not downsizing although it is often misunderstood to be so. It is not restructuring. It changes the work process and work itself; wasteful and useless work is curtailed. Some jobs are merged, even important jobs are created.

Re-engineering contemplates on:

- re-thinking on the fundamentals;
- breakthrough in mind-set;
- simplifying the multi-activity chart;
- radical redesigning of business process.

Only applying re-engineering technique will not yield high performance unless there is willingness and competency of individual employees. The process of re-engineering involves:

- Move towards horizontal instead of vertical;
- Organise by process instead of function;
- Manage as leaders and coaches instead of supervision;
- Empowerment;
- Making jobs result-oriented instead of activity-oriented.

Shooting into future through re-engineering is almost like space rocket—excess burden is to be discarded although many may feel sentimental that they had contributed for building in initial stage of organisation (which has now become a load).

Organisation re-engineering does not mean only redesigning of structure but alignment of structure, management processes, information systems, reward systems and people. RE integrates the purpose, process and people. In re-engineered organisations people gain greater prestige and importance. It does not push growth rather removes the factors limiting the growth. HR professional, therefore need to develop an all encompassing vision.

Re-engineering the Human Capital

(a) At Micro Level

Goethe said "Treat a man as he is, and he will remain as he is; treat a man as he can and should be, and he will become as he should be". Unless one believes in the unseen human potential there will only be status quo. Man is the index and the foundation too. Man stands on the threshold of a big change. Man is the maker of his own destiny. 'One must not treat human nature like a machine. A great plasticity is needed in dealing with its complex motives" said Sri Aurobindo, the great prophet and yogi. Every advancement begins in a small way and with the individual only. Development of man is the only means for the formation of a perfect society.

Man is to rise above his self-limiting interest to the level of good man, a satisfied man with broad outlook. Man is a technological animal, thus he is something called homo faber, man the maker. Man has evolved to a point where he can alter consciously and radically, himself, his biological make-up, his physical environment and particular and nature in general.

It is unfortunate that we are standing at such a pedestal today where everybody speaks about a successful man; nobody speaks about an ethical man, a moral man, a cultural man. Nobody seems to have difficulties in setting priorities but in setting posteriorities i.e. on what should not be done.

Upgrading the quality of existing people using communication and technology appropriately. Through information networking, video-conferencing, telecommunication etc. this liability can be transformed into an asset. Employees' self renewal is necessary through a 6-dimensional personal growth which will facilitate reengineering the mind set:

- spiritual;
- aesthetic;
- intellectual;
- psychological;
- material;
- physical.

Quantitative human stock-taking in organisation such as cost per employee, net profit per employee, output per employee are necessary as a pre-requisite to human re-engineering. What is more important is optisizing (how many people do we need who should stay) rather than downsizing (how many to get rid off who must go).

Knowledgeable managers are many. Their knowledge may be without utility. Meaningful knowledge for business success is the requirement, it is industrial knowledge. Knowledge analysis is crucial. It asks certain diagnostic questions like:

- do we have the right knowledge?
- is our knowledge progressing?

- are we paid for the knowledge we contribute?
- is our knowledge built into goods and services?
- how can we improve further?
- are we missing something?

(b) At Macro Level

Long term investment on improving quality of human capital is a very important element in competitiveness. Priorities which help organisation to expand are:

- long term over quick solution;
- convention over convenience;
- effort over comfort;
- sublimation over diversion;
- confrontation over appeasement;
- agreement at higher level over conflict.

Strategically restructuring the systems and structures with a purpose and equipping people in the organisation with the required skill and knowledge is what amounts to re-engineering at macro level. A large number of jobs at shop floor and in the office will be rendered obsolete. Some part of the workforce will adapt itself to new technology but others cannot keep pace.

With successive doses of promotion we lose loyal people, those who get promoted slowly become incompetent. Everybody rises to his level of incompetence. Before mushrooming of incompetent people all around, promotion policy requires radical change like abolishing positional titles and instead giving more money, responsibility and status etc. Interestingly of one meritorious is not promoted, many are disillusioned and de-motivated. And the non-deserving promoted case feels reassured about his lobby and opportunism. Organisations get saddled with such wrong men in wrong places. Can there be everlasting sense of achievement for individuals in organisations.

Promotion need not be the only reward. To accommodate aspirations of people against levels have risen to 15 against prescribed 3-5 irrespective of organisational needs. As a result people do only the same job at four levels. The pyramids have taken demotions through promotions. Dictated promotions are prevalent. The favoured few who get promotions really do not (or cannot) do more than what they were doing before. They are just promoted for higher positional title only. Each time a person is promoted, his/her job is downgraded.

Counter productive or dysfunctional hierarchy is meaningless; 3-layers of doers, supervisors and the planners is enough. Management by all employees has the key to efficiency. Instead of criticizing and reporting a problem there should be suggestions along with to solve. Everybody is aware of the present condition of the organisation and business environment. CFT (cross functional teams) are horizontal threads while hierarchical structures act as vertical threads adding strength to the cloth. Over a period of time every executive works in a number of CFTs and there is cultural transformation, the culture moves towards an OCTAPACE culture which stands for openness, confrontation, trust, authenticity, pro-activity, autonomy, collaboration and experimentation.

Human beings can make or break an organisation. An organisation is not built out of money but out of people. It survives through:

- Empowerment;
- Trusteeship;
- Enthusiasm;
- Networks;
- Multidisciplinary teams;
- Pro-activity;
- Core-growth;
- Self-propelled knowledge-workers;
- Changing mindset.

However there are number or ogranisational irritants too viz. passing the buck, poisoning the boss's ears, lobbying and groupism, repetitive and unsystematic activities, man-made bypasses to manage ups and downs, poor delegation and high expectation etc. They are needed to be overcome. Through retraining in multi-skilling, quality consciousness, team work, empowerment, attitudinal change, restructuring etc. these irritants can be straightened.

Pagey Ullas has classified organisations into 4 types so that to identify our own, they are:

Dinosaur: Hydra-headed monster. De-ossification is required to make these lean, efficient, resilient, agile otherwise these will die. Huge bureaucratic, seldom believe in learning development.

Zen: Means radical consciousness. Tremendous learning abilities. Capable of change by challenging themselves. Vision oriented. Empowering and participative.

Aggressive: Opposes anything new, against system.

Reactive: Rises slowly to external change.

Stephen Covey in the Seven Habits of Effective People Writes, "so often the problem is in the system, not in the people; if you put good people in bad systems, you get bad results".

Making the Future Happen Now

Seneca said in 58AD, "First we must seek what it is that we are aiming at, then we must look about for the road by which we can reach it most quickly". When our processes are a mess and we automate we get an automated mess only, nothing else. We must demonstrate that we are still capable of creative regeneration and that we can develop a new path into the future that stands before us in all its mystery and majesty. Learning to see underlying structures rather than events is of crucial importance. Repositioning people, rethinking strategies will be the important functions to be ensured. Constructing human network and information network helps in catching human nerve.

Concern for quality should bridge the difference between union and management, staff and line, operation and maintenance etc. Openness, egalitarianism, informality, consensus based decision making, learning by doing etc. are to be imbibed. We must give importance to the things that unite and ignore as much as possible those that separate.

Harmony between the idea and system, harmony between understanding, acceptance and practice, harmonizing all divergent and conflicting elements within himself and the organisation are to be practised. The shift of the concept from personnel management to human resource management is the first step in adopting a larger perspective.

Man must aim at developing an integrated man, a spiritual man, a perfect man and individual. Such an individual will be constituting the future society. Organisations will be required to fulfil contradictory requirement like to be innovative and efficient simultaneously. Strategic reconciliation is to be made between seemingly conflicting goals like:

- thinking long term whilst delivering short term results;
- investing in innovation while increasing operational efficiency;
- between separation and connection;
- competition and collaboration among teams.

Learning society is taking over very fast. It will be post-capitalist society. Organisations will be required to understand how to master knowledge work i.e. to create knowledge, to exploit knowledge, to apply knowledge to get best form of knowledge fast and logically. Net and RE the mindset do influence business drastically. Most executives are the monarchs of the 'present they are incapable to give neither sufficient time nor thought to the future. Futuristic executives must be identified to prepare for the emerging paradigm. Such executives accept the responsibility of making the future happen. Making the future is not to decide what should be done tomorrow but what should be done today to have a tomorrow. They will be the masters of team work, they will be leaders who will delegate to their team members and individual hero concept will be a passe.

Transformational and transactional leaders to be discovered at appropriate areas while re-engineering HR. Transformational leaders are capable of changing values. They inspire through individual attention to the followers. They form self-propelled teams. Transactional leaders rely on practical guidance. They clarify roles, expectations for followers etc.

Epilogue

The words of wisdom of Chuang Tzu (disciple of Lao Tzu) was, "Be careful not to interfere with the natural goodness of the heart of man. Man's heart may be forced down or stirred up. In each case the issue is fatal". Living systems must change themselves as they adapt to change in environment like a self-organising biological species. Talent retention through work-fun is needed. Small islands in organisations may be created to innovate, experiment, dream in an unrestrained manner. It adds value to organisation.

Hierarchies, rigid structures, tasks are changing. There is flexi-time with round the clock accessibility to the work place. Individual tasks is being replaced by project work. Cross-divisional transfers are common. CEO's instead of top notch will be central executive officer. Quantum restructuring is on: deconstruct or be deconstructed. Discarding outdated axioms is the need of the hour.

Through constructive dissent knowledge workers will don the role of teachers. This will facilitate through leaders who shall bring visionary, strategic and global perspective to the decision making process. Sense of fulfillment is coming from the quality of work life (QWL). Our action is to integrate technological social, human, organisational and societal demands.

In fact men and machines are becoming actual extensions each other. Let us not be victims of our own sophistication.

5

Management in New Social Order

The Root is Man

The root is man. Behaviour is a series of acts through which man moves in time and space. It is a datum of observation but a datum that does not constitute a self-evident fact. Instead it is a fact that is given meaning by the observer in the very process of observation.

Man is basically a defining animal. Definitions unrelated to the behaviour of man in politics or in any other area of human activity have no content. Whatever meaning a physical scientist gives to his object(s) of study they don't talk back to him but the living man does mind and talk back to the scientist.

Interpersonal relations have behavioural patterns, which may be stable and simple or otherwise. From such pattern emerges either "power" or "conflict". Examples are economic power, political power, racial conflict, rivalries etc.

Groups, organisations or nations have no independent status apart from the conduct of the individual who are related [illegible] behaving towards each other in certain ways. But this does [illegible] mean that these are not real and meaningful units having str[illegible] function of their own. Undoubtedly they are real. R[illegible] organisation, institution, states and nation cannot be de[illegible] we speak of verdict of court, decision of bureau, action of legislature etc., theses is nothing but due to human beings who decide, opine or act.

For studying any aspect of human behaviour, which is only part of his existence as a total human being, attention must be given to the social martix of political behaviour. Man is socially related to other men in a variety of ways that make him a total human being.

Of what use to man is his economic behaviour, his athletic behaviour or his artistic behaviour? The behaviour itself is shaped directly by the needs, drives, predispositions or fears and hopes of the individual actor. The man behind the surface personality is consciousness: an important area of research. Friedrich Nietzsche, German philosopher had asked: Do you really believe that the sciences would ever have originated and grown if the way had not been prepared by magicians, astrologers, alchemists and witches whose promises and pretensions first had to create the thirst, a hunger and a taste for the hidden and the forbidden powers?

Today's Man

Man lives between two truths-the truth of the past and that of the future. There is the third truth of constantly moving from past to the future. Sri Aurobindo considers man the mental being, as a transitory being, he is not the last rung of the evolutionary process.

Frans de Waal writes in The Chimpanzee Politics (1982) that monkeys are our colonial cousins. There is similarity of behaviour; they conduct their violent transactions on treetops, we in board rooms. Our corporate life, like that of monkeys is shaped by unstable power structures and status hierarchies based on [illegible]tructive competitions.

[illegible]velopment in terms of thinking feeling and willing is of [illegible]ortance. Difficulties begin with definitions as it commits [illegible]ts. Definitions must be operational and must be [illegible]ally instead of jugglery of words. Rightly said Dr. [illegible] are the victims of our own sophistications.

Role of man can be taken as a basic unit. If we don't know a person's role his behaviour appears to be enigmatic. A role is used as a conceptual tool on three kinds of behavioural analysis—social, cultural and personal. Role lays bare the inter-relatedness and inter-dependence of people. Political changes can now be observed at the level of individual actor but the political intention cannot be inferred fully.

With the turn of the century we have to have a management with a difference. In the incoming times man may stand nowhere. He will be reduced to a personnel with staff number only, a commodity which will be motivated through payment. Once unserviceable he will be discarded. Must technological advance swell man's ego and shrink his conscience? Man needs to take pause from his breathless pursuit and see where he is actually heading.

Today we are standing on the pedestal what science has made for us. We don't talk about a moral, a culture, a thoughtful man but surely speak about a successful man. Our life has become faster and outlook result-oriented and materialistic. All sensory organs have become new commercialism. Slowly man and machine are becoming actual extensions of each other.

Challenges Before Behaviourists

The behaviourists are neither wide-eyed prophets nor blind apostles. Behaviourists not only study the individual as a unit but also as a small group, a organisation, a community, a mass movement, a nation may be the focus of behavioural enquiry; and events structures, functions, processes or relations may serve as a category of behavioural analysis.

As long as there is talk about man's common humanity, just as there is talk about man's in-humanity to man, the behavioural scientist cannot escape the task of determining what is human and what is not.

There may be covert or overt patterns, which are of crucial importance. How these patterns have come about and how they are transmitted are questions of considerable interest to the analysts of behaviour. These patterns may be cumulative results of learning and are transmitted from generation to generation in the process of socialisation. The patterns may be adaptations to the environment in which a group lives.

Ways of intuitions will be of crucial significance to handle an unpredictable, unusual, rapidly changing situation. Can intuition be fully developed? It is challenging question for a behaviourist to find ways and to judge its accuracy and efficiency.

The discrepancy between what a man is doing and what he thinks he is doing: this dilemma need not be the observer's dilemma as the observer has the advantage over the observed: he can check his own meanings against the observed.

The problem of reducing error in the behavioural science is compounded by the complexity of human behaviour. The smallest observable unit of behaviour, the act, is inordinately complex, even if treated as a biological, or neurological phenomenon. How much more complex is the series of acts that constitutes the behaviour of the human organism as a whole! And this complexity is compounded when we come tc deal with man's behaviour in his social relations. The observer's task would almost seem hopeless if it were not for one significant aspect of human behaviour: the fact that man himself gives meaning to his multiple action. Otherwise observation itself becomes meaningless. Observation is itself a form of behaviour that involves in giving certain type of meaning to the object of observation, depending on who the observer is.

Perceptions may or may not correspond to reality but as the determination of reality is elusive, they serve as substitutes. If X perceives Y as influential: X may behave well towards Y as if Y were in fact influential. If X finds out that Y is not or less so, then what X expected, X may have misbehaved with identifiable consequences like cognizable offences. Undoubtedly attribution of influences are based on just such experiences and for that reason too, constitute' definitions of the situation' that have a very real existence of their own and therefore, are proper objects of behavioural investigation. Interestingly even a situation that is misperceived may be real in its consequences.

In human enterprise science cannot investigate values and preferences of men nor can it tell which goal is the best or what action is just. Therefore any scientific study of human behaviour will be inter-subjectively consensual rather that subjectively philosophical notions about man. Any intellectual treason on the part of a behaviourist may harm himself as his works serves the ultimate goal that is man.

John Heider writes in The Tao of Leadership that all behaviour contains certain opposites:

- Hyper-inflation leads to collapse.
- A show of strength shows insecurity.
- What goes up must comes down.
- If you want to prosper be generous.

Also:

- The feminine outlasts the masculine.
- The feminine allows, but the masculine causes.
- The feminine surrenders, then encompasses and wins.

And:

- Water wears away the rock.
- Spirit overcomes force.
- The weak will undo the mighty.

It is wise to learn and see things backwards, inside out and upside down as interesting facts are revealed.

The Goal too is Man

Man disagrees on the nature of man. Which is the man in whose service the applied behavioural science is devoted to?

Is he an evolving man?

Is he a just man?

Is he democratic man?

Is he a man to be controlled as he is brutish?

Is he is a man in transition to dignity and liberation?

In fact it is for the man as a whole entity. Human perfectibility is the future of man. Evolving a conscious human relationship into a creative unity and harmony will be the future of man. That un-negotiable fissure in human personality is to be overcome. Development of man is the first condition for the formation of a perfect society. He is our index and our foundation too.

Man as such is an imperfact being—his mind is only in an evolutionary stage heading for perfection. Management therefore instead of words, should by actions care for human development. Man is not a mass of flesh, bones, blood-water conglomerate only. "One must not treat human nature like a machine to be handled according to rigid mental rules—a great plasticity is needed in dealing with its complex motives" said Aurobindo.

New Social Order and Goodwork

A new social order is inevitable and management has to be transformed towards, social commitment. Western management thought has given us management "by objective", "by performance", "by result", etc. but the hub of all these is the Man who needs to be developed through continuous enrichment and activation. This only shall grow a universal truth which will refine man to guide mankind in the process.

Inter-institutional analysis from behavioural point of view is also relevant. The behaviour has politics ingrained in it. The relationship between institution and behaviour is necessarily complementary. In fact institutional arrangements, norms or functions express behavioural patterns that have been stabilised through passage of time.

Like science and technology knowing its present limits it cannot predict its future limits; the behavioural technology too expands as per its amenability to scientific technology advancements. The most important aspect of culture is that its existence is predicted on the existence of another culture. One culture always constitutes the environment for the another. Awareness of different cultures sensitises us to the culture, in which we live, act think, feel and judge. Otherwise we are culture bounded: we do not know who we are not why. Culture is a mental construct abstracted from the behaviour of people and their works.

A full and well-appointed life is now desirable for man living in society but on condition that it is a true and beautiful life. Therefore in the modern commercial age, the soul may linger a while for some petty gains and experiences but could not permanently rest. If it is persisted too long, life would become clogged and perish. Like the too massive Titan it will collapse by its' own mass, *mole ruet sua*. Hence man must be chisell to become a mental being. Management must aim at developing and integrated man, a spiritual man, a perfect man and individual. Such an 'individual' will be constituting the future society.

For those who disagree violently the Mother has said, 'For all to agree, each must rise to the top of his consciousness, it is on the heights that harmony is created. When we have to work collectively it is always better to insist in our thoughts, feelings and actions, on points of disagreements rather than on the points of difference. We must give importance to the things that unite and ignore as much as possible those separate'. That is, coming to agreement is the only way to do goodwork.

To be earth citizen is to go beyond the present frontiers of consciousness which fragment everything and also divides the outer from the inner. In order to nurture human spirit this division is to be transcended so that the humanity continually faces new challenges and there is continual renewal, a continual beginning. Born of the universe we cannot narrow our loyalties, belonging to humanity nothing human can be alien to us. On this small planet earth there is no room for permanent enemies and alienations. Saving life not only of all humans but of all species is much more important than the defence of borders. Management can be development of Man (free individual): the first condition of the formation of a perfect society.

Management

Sri Aurobindo said, "Freedom is the highest law and last consummation". An individual committed to the central aim of an organisation and identified with it, should be given freedom to err as well as succeed, for only so can he and the organisation grow. He has also written that all problems of nature are essentially problems of harmony. Every living organism depends on the smooth harmonious interaction and co-operation of its composite parts for growth and survival. Harmony in organisation is not confined only to co-operative relations among employees or between employees and management. Harmony is to be between the idea, the system or schemes for executions and the actual outer expression. Harmony between understanding, acceptance and practice, harmonising all divergent and conflicting elements within himself and organisation are required.

A relationship can be maintained only as long as the participants are in agreement as to what each actor must or must not do in the performance of his role. If there is disagreement over what kind of behaviour should be expected, the relationship is likely to disintegrate.

The shift of the concept from Personnel Management to Human Resource Management is the first step in adopting a larger perspective. The inherent preferences of organisations are clarity, certainty and perfection. The inherent nature of human relationship involves ambiguity, uncertainty and imperfection. How one honours, balance and integrates the needs of both is the real trick of management.

Life never stands still, if we do not progress we regress. Progress is not an end in itself as it is considered to be, rather it means a constant effort to upgrade one's ideas, services, employees and systems.

Unfree people like immature children are difficult to manage; but free and responsible are easy to manage. All management involves commanding and obeying. But in a democracy, all commanding, all commanding should avoid injuring self-respect of the one commanded, and all obeying should be on the basis of one's freedom and self-respect, and never degrade into cringing.

Machines and computers only do not make business a success: it is the people. Similarly no theory or plan will make business a success than can only be done with people. Technology makes things possible but it is the people who make it happen. Man is thus the primary input to the management process. A few examples of priorities which help organisations to expand are:

- Long term over quick solution
- Convention over convenience
- Effort over comfort
- Submission over diversion
- Confrontation over appeasement
- Agreement at higher level over conflict.

Materialistic management is an offshoot of western methods has done more harm than good in certain areas. Management blames workers for non-cooperative outlook despite fat salary and perks, workers feel aggrieved against management for having reduced them as their puppets or tools of production process. Lack of belongingness, absence of fellow-feeling, divide rule policy within organisation is an obvious result of pernicious form of western management system which has been disregarding the human approach so far. This has led to demoralisation among workers and society has suffered. Although the management's efforts are full it suffers from mental unrest due to labour trouble, market recession etc. Materialistic management of western style will not help as it is "soulless" and fresh thinking is now necessary as to the objective, scope and content of management thinking in India.

Man is much more than a mere wage earner and keeping in view his self-development and social responsibility management thoughts need refined rewritten. Western hierarchy of needs may have an analogous structure where all needs are equally important and go together. Incentives and rewards may not be enough for motivation; soul satisfaction will be the necessity in future. Management will overcome the straight-jacket career-discipline structure and man will be developed in an integrated form—a good man, a noble man, a cooperative man with broad national outlook instead of narrow self-limiting interests.

New Age Man

Man stands on the threshold of a big change. It is the change of consciousness, a new approach to life itself to meet the requirements of the future. In his crucible of fleeting existence man is being moulded in the image of his soul.

Dr. Rupert Sheldrake has advocated theory of Morphogenetic field (1968) stating that all living organisms contribute to he "memory pool" even after the expiry of the species. It means characteristics of species are not limited to the physical chemistry of DNA since a transcendent factor functions as an over-riding mechanism exercising some form of control over future intra-species behaviour. There is interesting evidence that the children pick up seamlessly, the rudiments of personal computer (PC) and information technology (IT) and are faster too than their counterparts of the previous generation. Computer interface has become inherent trait in newborns.

A new list of action-points for humble daily practice:

- Consecrate physical objects, institution
- Consecrate organisational hierarchy
- Consecrate systems and sub-systems
- Consecrate each human being
- Consecrate in detail the life and growth of organisation
- Enter into personal conscious relationship with everyone and nourish them with your consciousness
- Remove avoidable sources in interpersonal frictions
- Set the machines and the systems in quiet rythmic working order
- Consciously maximise the efficiency of subsystems and systems
- Handle outer and inner activities as quickly as possible
- Nurture receptive atmosphere
- However little it may be initiative positive improvement instead of justifying status quo.

Sri Aurobindo's prophetic pronouncement can be taken as a guiding force for the behaviourists. "...for when the material circumstances favour a great change but the heart and mind of the race are not really ready-especially the heart, failure may be predicted, unless indeed men are wise in time and accept the inner change alongwith the external readjustments". With massive information jamming managers will be required to take decisions in complex situations where either complete data is unmanageable or unavailable or too costly. Therefore only "left brain" style of logical and analytical approach will not do and one has to blend analysis with insights.

6

Management Facing A New World

A Cue from Kautilya

Kautilya's *Arthashastra* not only deals with statecraft but also contains a number of timeless ideas that modern managers may find useful. The author indicates that *arjana* (acquisition), *vardhana* (growth) and *rakshana* (conservation) are three very important aspects of the *artha* (economy), whether it be the economy of a nation or that of an industry. The Arthashastra sees four aspects of man in his relationship to the world and to the economy:

— Man is the Shaper of his own destiny;

— Man is the one who can change work situations;

— Man is the Exploiter of resources, both material and human;

— Man is the Corruptible in his weaker moments.

To get the best out of human beings working together in an organisation, Kautilya emphasized the need to test the following competencies before assigning responsibilities to each: technical capability, intelligence, perseverance, dexterity, eloquence, boldness, presence of mind, ability to face crises, uprightness, firmness and concern in dealing with others and strength of character. Today, it is an everyday practice that before initiating any serious action a manager undertakes some kind of CINE, that is assessment of the controllable internal and non-controllable external factors. This is quite in consonance with the wisdom of Kautilya.

Technology and Man

In today's society, science and technology determine the direction of social change. The speed of these changes is accelerating and the area of their impact is broadening, while the nature of the changes is becoming more sophisticated, due to rapidly changing technology. Technological change, if properly managed, could become self-propagating and a way of life. It will then no longer need to be stimulated but will happen spontaneously. A professional needs to keep pace with change, or he ceases to be a professional and rapidly becomes an outdated fossil. Even values change with the changing times. Thus ecology has become a value which nobody can neglect today.

Technology can be understood as an expression of the relationship between input and output where the two basic components are: hardware (machinery and tools) and software (human skill and know-how). The relative significance of the two components varies with the type of industry which can be labour-intensive, capital-intensive, technology-intensive or brain-intensive. Technological advancement has always been related to the impact it produces on society, through the service it renders to humankind in terms of a significant improvement in the quality of life of large numbers of people, the enhancement of human dignity and a greater realisation of human potential.

The process of absorption, assimilation and final acceptance of new technology by society is slow. It is often resisted and provokes scepticism and cynicism. Ultimately only the perceptible and the quantifiable gains accruing to large numbers of people will convince society of the value of any new technology. It is then accepted only because of the actual benefits obtained and never simply because it is new. Whenever technology has brought disaster and death, society has raised its voice of protest and has discarded such technology. Examples of beneficent technology are numerous: fax machines, copiers, high definition television, cellular telephones, breeding of high yielding grain varieties. On the other hand some technological developments now on the way out because of the harm they have done are D.D.T., supersonic aircraft, CFC gases like Freon as refrigerants.

Man and Development

Development is a matter of human energies rather than of economic wealth. Japan is a striking example. It lacks all other resources except a valuable human resource. Japan has used this resource for its amazing economic growth. No wonder the slogan common in all Japanese industries is "Japan has no other wealth except its people". Because this is not just a slogan, but a central belief of Japanese managers, a number of human resource development practices special to Japan have evolved. Some of these are: stress on life-long service, the importance given to seniority, continuous human development programmes, consultation and consensus ("ringi") in arriving at decisions, emphasis on total quality and on *kaizen* or continuous improvement.

Management of Human Resources

All these are management practices. Clearly, it is management that makes the difference. Peter Drucker (1974) once stated: "It can be said without too much over-simplification that there are no 'underdeveloped countries' only undermanaged' ones. Japan, a hundred years ago, was an underdeveloped country by every material measurement and now it is the most developed of all the countries. Clearly enlightened management is the key requirement for real development to take place".

In the past, the management of human resources primarily focused on getting the maximum work out of people, in return for an adequate compensation and welfare package, a *quid pro quo* of sorts. Today it is realised that for the effective management of change of the problems and opportunities associated with it, it is necessary to view the personnel itself as constituting the organisation, and not merely as one of the resource inputs. Human begins are highly sensitive to the importance attached to them, and it is possible for them to achieve wonders, once the perception sinks in that they actually matter'.

Technology comes not from nature, but from man. Alfred Russell Wallace (1983) (co-discoverer with Darwin of evolution) said, "Man is the only animal capable of directed and purposeful evolution, he makes tools". Technology, therefore, is nothing but an extension of man's tool-making ability.

Information Revolution and Renewal of the Human Engine

The most striking aspect of technology which has revolutionalized the modern world is in the field of electronics namely the information revolution. This has resulted in the fact that individuals are today no longer in any specific nation but are rather members of a 'transnation'. In this situation, the 'right' size of a task will become central. Is this task best done by a bee, a humming-bird, a mouse or an elephant? This is the question that has to be asked. All of them are needed, but each has a different task and a different ecology.

The traditional organisation believed in maximising each task in the conviction that efficiency required this. In an information-based organisation each task is measured in accordance with the real need. This is the principle behind the "just-in-time" concept of Japan. Instead of maintaining a large inventory of components, operations are fine-tuned so as to ensure that each component is delivered (and paid for) only at the moment it is actually required in the assembly line.

Similarly the human potential in an organisation also needs to be continually developed through well *tailored* 'skill-in-action' and 'quest for perfection' programmes. The present human resources development (HRD) function has to be repositioned if it is going to achieve all these objectives.

Need for Transformational Leadership

To achieve all this today's organisation requires a new type of leadership which is generally called transformational leadership. A transformational leader is one who possesses *charisma,* that is he is a visionary and is able to transmit to others his own vision of the company and its mission today and tomorrow. He is *inspirational,* that is he inspires trust and is capable of conveying important purposes in simple ways. Third a transformational leader offers *intellectual stimulation* to others and thus provides them with challenges in their life and work. Yet he is capable of giving *individual consideration*, attention and advice to others. His employees are not an anonymous mass but individual persons whom he knows and values. A transformational leader is a person who holds *clear, well known values* which he will not sacrifice. Such a person *empowers* and builds people up. He does not seek to dominate and pull others down. For him, authority does not exist for the benefit of the one who holds it. Rather it exists for the benefit and welfare of those who are subject to it. Thus the transactional leader recognises that a constituent confers authority on a manager, not the other way round. Constituents can be employees, customers, shareholders, the public, the consumers and suppliers, in a word stakeholders.

The *credibility* of a manager will define his effectiveness, as a Transformational leader. To develop credibility, a manager needs to practise six exercises. He needs to discover himself, appreciate his constituents and their diversity, affirm the shared values of the organisation, develop his own capacity, have a clear purpose and sustain the hope and optimism of others.

Developing Human Resources

In the fast-changing world of today, it is not surprising that people tend to get bored with the repetitive tasks that a normal job implies and boredom leads to inefficiency and poor quality work. Now human beings constitute the essential infrastructure for all growth and development. In the ultimate analysis it is people who build (or demolish) an organisation. Unfortunately amidst preoccupations with material resources, managers give human resources a back seat in their concerns, ultimately causing inefficiencies and failure.

For these reasons several well known methods have been devised to overcome boredom and create a greater sense of enthusiasm in work.

Job enrichment is the first. This is the effort to increase or vary the content of any job. A simple method of achieving this is through job rotations. One may cite the example of the celebrated Pohang Steel Company (POSCO) in Pohang, South Korea. This is the world's biggest single steel works producing 28 millions tons of steel a year, all with imported iron ore and coal. It is also one of the most efficient plants which manufactures high quality steel at the lowest price with a total work force of less than 10,000 people. (By comparison TISCO, with equally modern equipment, produces 3 million tones with 35,000 workers). Clearly the productivity of POSCO workers is very high, and no wonder, since the company's slogan is "Natural Resources Limited, Human Ingenuity Unlimited". This is why the company regularly rotates skilled personnel. This has not created any problems, rather, it has groomed 'technical saints'. Not surprisingly, for job enrichment shows a person that he is a productive member of the organisation, making a valued contribution and this boosts his self-esteem and pride in work.

Also, a major part of the workforce is normally capable of exercising far more initiative, responsibility and creativity than their present jobs require or allow. These capabilities represent untapped resources which at present are being wasted. Particularly important are the creativity and the capacity for responsible, self-directed, self-controlled behaviour.

Means must, therefore, be tried to empower people and enable them to take initiatives and make decisions at their own levels. This may require some risk taking on the part of the management, but it usually produces disproportionately good results.

Senior management is usually aware where the company is going; but tends not to know just where the organisation actually is. The rest of the personnel is usually familiar with the current state of affairs, but does not know what direction to take in the future. HRD repositioning will help give management a sense of reality and personnel a sense of importance by getting them to jointly diagnose the actual state of the organisation and to articulate a vision for the future.

Skills for Managers

Managers have often to break the circle of ineffectiveness. Either they have to fire the low performers and hire better personnel or they can respond to low performers with high expectations. The first is not practical, at least in India, and the second appears to several managers to involve too great a risk. Hershey and Blanchard (1977) have identified two different cycles that managers can use to maximise the task relevant maturity of employees: the Developmental Cycle and the Regressive (or Disciplinary) Cycle. The developmental cycle isa growth cycle where managers attempt to increase the task relevant maturity of an individual or a group beyond the level they had ever previously reached.

In the regressive cycle, the manager deliberately and with planned foresight, makes a disciplinary intervention when a subordinate behaves less maturely than is expected of him. In the development cycle, a manager, dealing with an employee who has displayed maturity and reliability tries to raise him still higher by development interventions, that is, by giving him further responsibility, allowing him more initiative and showing he has high expectations from the person. In other words, in dealing with personnel, managers, must be flexible and use a leadership style appropriate to the level of maturity of each person. This, of course, is easier said than done, but managers must at least bear this matter in mind. John Locke (1927) spoke about an important requirement for success in all interpersonal relations, that is *'pattern recognition'*. This is a mental ability to recognise the different types of personalities one has to deal with. The same gift is required to perceive correctly the situation one is faced with.

In our daily life we constantly use pattern recognition while distinguishing different types of music, personality traits, detecting loopholes and fallacies and so forth. All these acts involve a logical sequence of mental operations which the human mind performs subconsciously. When using pattern recognition in dealing with people, we must not forget certain simple points.

— One does not know a friend only from his conversation but from having dealings with him. Human relations are judged by praxis, rather than by theories.

— When public reactions are taken as a fact-or-for recognising a pattern, it should be remembered that public reactions are only a wayward nymph dancing on uncertain feet.

— Triumph of the good and the surge of evil are sometimes inexplicable.

Another important point is that, whether acting in the regression or the developmental mode, managers have to consider the degree of emotion to be used, so as not to produce either excessive self confidence or excessive anxiety. Inappropriate use of either style will, of course do harm.

The Synergistic approach to interpersonal relations involves achieving a whole that is greater than its parts put together. The kind of synergy that is desirable in organisations is the one that binds working teams together and helps them function at a much higher level of efficiency and enthusiasm. It helps in achieving better results and has significant influence on the behaviour of individuals and groups. Synergy is action-oriented and highly contagious energy which is latent in all working teams and everyone in a position of command is responsible for unleashing this energy and taking advantage of its potential.

Remaking Managers

Uncertainties are on the rise due to a fundamental restructuring of the economy and of Indian society. Today companies sometimes seem more like 'functioning anarchies' than like the bureaucracies of the pervious decades. In today's situation the human engine of renewal needs unlearning and then learning anew. Responding to the future rather than reacting to the past is today's password.

Alvin Toffler (1985) writes, "the new technology is driving us not towards an Orwellian world of robotised, standardised, monotonic societies but towards the most highly differentiated social structures in history, each of which produces its own transient sub-systems of values within the larger framework of society". The manager of tomorrow has to operate in a changing environment having certain clear characteristics:

- We shall function in a society demanding a more democratic approach;
- Decentralisation will be the keyboard in larger organisations;
- The information explosion will completely change the way we think;
- We face the challenging task of dealings with a better educated work force;
- The insatiable desire for more consumer goods will provide over greater business opportunities;
- Younger managers will be more exposed to machine-language and need a greater fiscal-orientation in their mental set-up;
- Automation will invade the office, the home and public life;

In this new setup the successful manager will need certain characteristics:

- He will be a manager of change which he will have to anticipate;
- He will need the power of strategic thinking to integrate region with nation;
- He will need to recognise the world beyond the office and face its challenges;
- He will have to understand the goals of society;
- He will be an educator of others about the nature of change;
- He will have to see people as potential and strategic resources and groom them accordingly;
- He will require a sound grounding in management and related disciplines;
- He will need sensitivity to corporate as well as national cultural traits;

— He will need skill in dealing with government;

— He will have to instinctively use a sound information-base in his decision making;

— He will require to be computer literate;

— He must be capable of a transnational outlook and possess communication skills;

— He must nurture a belief in the 'value-adding' role of managers;

— He will need to be a person with known and practised values.

Such managers are not born. They can only be produced by great emphasis on and a new understanding of the science of Human Resource Development.

7

Business, Spirituality and Soulwork

Management With A Difference

Calculus of Spirituality and Soul Work

Spirituality is a private matter. So is attitude to work. Life, politics and business are inherently impure pursuits. It is fast, structured, profiteering and materialistic. Spirituality and work can be user friendly though they have so far been unfriendly.

There is no need of a temple or church or a masjid or a place of fire worship. Our earth, our building, our institution and organisations are no less. These are our places of work and worship too. There is no harm. I must repeat absolutely no harm in reading from a Sufi saint, referring a Tibetan health book or practice Zen meditation. Work is worship is an age-old saying. This worship is not a religious kind of ritual. It is meaningful. A Hebrew word *'avodah'* means both work and worship. At the root there cannot be any division between work and worship provided one realises this truth.

In industries we have heard of work for work sake, sincere work, effective work, smart work etc. but 'soul work' is something different from these. Working from one's soul is 'soul work'. Let us do what we can do fully, satisfying and soul-filling. Soulful activity can't be subversive, it can't be a detrimental activity. Now question arises if someone entrusts you with a work and you are not accepting, it is subversive to your soul. Let us not have too much to do. Soul work is nothing but a spirituo-management approach. That is possibly the real work.

There is no need to harp on work, work and work. Whenever we feel fatigued, frustrated we use the following expressions:

- — Hell to everything;
- — It is too much of a load of work;
- — Oh! Let me relax;
- — It is un-nerving;
- — It is horrible etc.

But how many of us have cared to listen to our heart? When we do that we get spiritual sustenance. All agitations in our mind pacifies. A natural and soulful approach to work is of crucial importance in contrast to routine duty to and fro to work-spot.

Spiritual awakening amongst the industrial masses is definitely a challenging job. Because this mass is bogged down by its own materialistic load. There is a rat race amongst careerist executives who sacrifice friendship, family, relatives for climbing the ladder of success. How many of us remember that one day we have to be back into the human chain down below at the grass-root whom we left uncared for while climbing in the limited arena of our career success? There is no doubt that any materialistic pursuit has to arrive at a dead end.

When we are in employment we work on the average 33.3 per cent of our time and may be even more in some cases. It is a considerable time that we spend in work. Can we not match our work-energy with universal energy? It is all there everywhere, within and outside. If we can understand this concept there can be sea change in our 'work-attitude' and the work place undergoes a transformation—it becomes more humane. Once the work place is made more humane there is fulfilment of soul. Let good human beings succeed in business. Let not so good human beings be replaced by good human beings.

By soul work people become:

— Conscientiously responsible for their actions;

— Self-suffering, non-dependence on others;

— Willing people listening to one another, extending helping hand;

— Caring for each other: employers caring for employees (work/industry).

Soul-work boosts productivity as well as soothes workers' psyche. Doing soul-work presupposes certain existential aspects:

— Who you are;

— Profile of your being;

— Your character in organisation;

— What you express through words or deeds;

— You and others.

Executive who does soul work look above their table top spreadsheet. They focus on:

— What is right and just;

— People;

— Values;

— Acting with compassion.

Aren't we working for systems, for people, for oneself? All these are reflections of nature i.e. part of a larger plan. It is a kind of seeing others by seeing oneself. Soulful working is a kind of self burnout.

Periodically one needs the following:

Return from	**Arrive at**
High speed movement	Silence
High energy activity	Inactivity
Hard driving world	Rest
Anxiety/cocktail hour	Peace/meditation

If there is a good to be found, it must be a spiritual good. And it is not too difficult to find it. In the new age economy those who are guided by the spiritual principles shall thrive, others will perish.

Compass of Business

It is the people who matter in the rise or fall of an industry or a business. People are the most intangible, the most complex element of any business equation. Employ a whole person not the labour part of a worker. The only way to reach people is to start by reaching into yourself by understanding yourself.

Use your own compass to see how far your intellectual and spiritual being interface with the issue. Assess your total psyche in the context of your work. Take soulful decisions. Ignoring 'who I am' and taking a business decision may be disastrous. Such decisions, if not quickly, may bear ill-fruits for the organisations any time during your tenure or later. Manage with a difference. Do you want to just keep doing what you are doing or work to excel incrementally? To be or to be better is the question.

In the work context firing people, punishing people, reprimanding people are not unethical, are not unjust. But it should be done conscientiously, not arbitrarily or conventionally. Those who underactive are different from those who can't do the job. Discrimination is not immoral. A worldwide segregation is on to separate evil from good, in politics, in business, in production etc. Organisations can be created.

It is a great error to overlook or to underestimate the effects of the 'modes of production' upon peoples lives. One must look deep into:

— how they produce; what they produce;

— why they work; where they live;

— whom they meet; how they meet;

— how they relax (recreate); what they eat;

— what they think (on freedom or slavery).

R.H. Tawney has spoken of straight forward hatred of a system that stunts personality and corrupts human relations by permitting the use of man by man as an instrument of pecuniary gain. Nothing is more destructive than destroying the peoples' understanding.

Integrating (or coalescing) spiritualism and work may be synergetic and lead to long lasting effects. Spirituality is the latest edge over modern management thinking and organisational behaviour. Through spiritualism and work higher performance at individual and organisational level can be achieved.

We all need a taste of the sublime, to lift our hearts to give us a hint of the infinite possibilities of life. Certain phenomena move, affect and connect humans in a very special manner but these are very difficult to explain through physical sciences. Self-remembering (Return to the self) is now up-coming very fast. Intellectual resources are engaged in this direction to create appropriate and suitable technology.

Work, Good Work and Stress

A job in which one finds no personal satisfaction destroys the soul. Mankind's physical and mental liberation is of crucial importance. Work is so central to human life that it is truly impossible to conceive of life at the human level without work. Albert Camus said "without work, all life goes rotten, but when work is soulless, life stifles and dies". It has been recognised in all authentic teachings of mankind that every human being born into this world has to work not merely to keep himself alive but to strive toward perfection. It is work which occupies most of the energies of human race.

Modern industrial society is immensely complicated, immensely involved, making immense claims on man's time and attention. The aim of modern industrialism is not to make work satisfying but to raise productivity. Its proudest achievement is labour-saving where by labour is stamped with the mark of undesirability. Thus what is undesirable cannot offer dignity; so the working life of a labourer is a life without dignity. There are safety regulations, claims of damages. No management is unaware of its duty to avoid accidents or physical conditions which impairs health. But workers' brains, minds and souls are altogether a different matter.

Everywhere the value of freedom, responsibility and human dignity have to be openly affirmed even where a neglect of these values would appear to allow the big industrial machine to run more smoothly and efficiently. It may not be possible to do without causing offence. To tell a young person that his personal integrity is more important than his career may sound almost like sabotage in the ears of the efficiency experts.

Paradoxical as it may seem, modern industrial society, in spite of an incredible proliferation of labour-saving devices, has not given people more time to devote their all-important spiritual tasks. This is perhaps the greatest evil. At the heart of our system of work lies our system of values and more precisely, our view of the individual and his relationships with others. Unless there are conscious efforts to the contrary wants will always rise faster than the ability to meet them. What could be more destructive than the destruction of peoples' understanding?

Good work is often ignored by the economic structure of the western world. Dr. EF Schumacher maintains that the purpose of man's work is three-fold:

- to produce necessary, useful goods and services;
- to enable us to use and perfect our gifts and skills;
- to serve and collaborate with other people in order to liberate inbuilt egocentricity.

Physical work even if strenuous does not absorb a great deal of power of attention, but mental work does. Both are however stressful. Stress comes from mechanics. Three types of stresses treated in mechanical engineering practice are:

— Tensile

— Comprehensive

— Torsional

It has a correspondence in human systems. An executive wanting to complete a target and runs into difficulty experiences tensile stress popularly known as tension). He is also under pressure from top management and therefore experience a comprehensive stress. In family matters the same executive pressurised by his family members viz. parents, wife, children to behave in a particular way to get into competition with neighbour thus developing torsional stress.

These three types of stress accumulate producing fatigue, stress and distortion in personality. Moreover most managements treat men as factors of production instead of responsible human persons which lead to innumerable stunted or even wasted lives with illness.

Office gossip, backbiting, affairs in office, bad mouth, berating, bribes, kickbacks, liquidation, politics, murder, hunger for power, suffering of innocents, rise or mediocre, less deserving elbowing one's way ahead etc. are quite common in today's business. To counter all these and today's stress you must:

— Keep your mind open

— Be attuned to people and ideas

— Slander none

— Be peace-loving

— Be considerate

— Listen others

— Listen yourself

Many people are interested in changing the way they live their lives. Spiritual matters like practise of silence, awareness of breathing, concentration, prayer in distress, an hour of silence with eyes closed defines a path of journey to discover oneself and a new man emerges. Today stretches ahead of me, waiting to be shaped. And here I am, the sculptor who gets to do the shaping. What today will be like is up to me. I get to choose what kind of day I will have.

Repositioning Man

There is a small saying: A person asked God, "What surprises you most about mankind?" God answered, "They lose their wealth to earn money; they lose their money to restore health; then by thinking anxiously about the future they forget the present; they neither live for the present nor the future; they live as if they will never die and they die as if they had never lived".

Man must live a life of his own. He should avoid monotonous life style. He should be satisfied with his own achievements and should not be jealous of others. But the truth is life is rarely exactly the way we want it to be. The people often do not act as we would like them to. Moment to moment there are aspects of life that we like and others that we don't. There always people who disagree with you do things differently. There are things that don't work out.

If you fight against the principle of life you will spend most of your life only in fighting battles. It is necessary to re-evaluate one's priorities otherwise lives will be spent only in fight about small things. Let there be a choice between:

- which battles are worth fighting;
- which should be left to themselves.

Adam Smith said, "The understanding of the great part of man are necessarily formed by his ordinary employments. A man whose life is spent in performing a few simple operation has no occasion to exert his understanding. He naturally loses, therefore the habit of such exertion. In every improved and civilized society this is the state into which the labouring poor, that is the great body the people, must necessarily fall, unless government takes some pains to prevent it". It is time to reposition man so that he can survive to reach the destiny of evolutionary process.

Epilogue

If not already, the management has to become proactive and knowledgeable. Clear sense of purpose for producing predictable results brings success to any effort. Similarly looking at business of life. I think it is possible to establish a rationale for taking the time to write a personal business plans for living our lives. Important life decisions have so far been reactive and short term, not proactive. Speaking from a materialistic point of view, industrial society, unless radically reformed must come to a bad end.

A young manager of 3rd millennium says:

"I don't want to join the rat race. Not be enslaved by machines, bureaucracies, boredom, ugliness. I don't want to become a moron, a robot, a commuter. I don't want to become fragment of a person. I want to do my own thing. I want to live relatively simply. I want to deal with people, not masks. People matter. Nature matters. Beauty matters. I want to be able to care". It is only an expression of longing for freedom. It is because freedom is totally lost.

8

Value-based Administration

Introduction

Empires, fall, ministers pass but bureaux remains. The administrative apparatus (bureaucracy) and the administrator define the governance and ensure its continuity. Peter Drucker once said in Japan, "It can be said without too much over-simplification that there are no 'underdeveloped countries'. There are only 'under-managed ones'. Japan, a hundred years ago, was an underdeveloped country by every material measurement and now it is the most developed of all the countries". It means, administration or management as the case may be, is the prime-mover and development is the consequence. Something more than mere inefficiency, redtape and rules have gone wrong. Essentially an administrator is to break the ineffective cycle.

Value: What It Is and Is Not

Value system is a holistic reality but is meaningful only with reference to a pattern or complex. Value merely perceived and/or conceived is valueless. It must be lived. Value system of administrators at various levels of hierarchy need not be similar and can differ. Value gaps or differences of values pertain to differences in conditions of life viz. age, sex, education, culture, religion and environmental conditioning; and thus there are variations in value system in each organisation.

New Public Management Approach (NPMA)

Peter Senge says in his book. The Fifth Discipline that there is a need to understand before one can predict and influence organisational events. Learning to see underlying structures rather than events is of importance. Every individual has some competency or other. If human competencies are not used, they do not get developed or sharpened. Natural resources limited, human ingenuity unlimited: use it. Ralph Waldo Emerson had rightly told, "People see only what they are prepared to see".

To add value to administration, and administrator is to:

— possess strategic thinking to integrate region with nation;

— recognise world beyond office and face its challenge;

— understand goals of society;

— see people as potential and strategic resources and goom them accordingly;

— be a party to desired evolutionary process at the very micro level;

— recource to information base in decision making;

— nurture belief in value adding;

— should be the shaper in his own area of activity and control.

Time has come to choose from:

— *Opacity:* Plethora of complex rules, compartmentalisation limited to only very few.

— *Transparency:* Established simple norms, massive flow of information across the interfaces.

Economists Finn Kydland & Ed Prescott asked whether policy needed to be rigid and rule-based; or relaxed based on ad hoc discretions. To which they had answered that there are areas where rule-based policy was better than discretion, and there were areas where discretionary methods yielded better results.

Hierarchies are being replaced by self-managing structures of various kinds: networks, multi-disciplinary teams, small action dyads etc.

Existing Maladies

Although administration in India has generally been criticised for its inefficient functioning, disproportionate delay intaking decisions, ineffective implementation of the decisions and a general lack of direction and purpose; but any strategy for controlling and developing administration are dependent to some extent on the acquiescence of the administrators involved and they resist it.

When the administrative culture changes very slowly, almost in negligible pace is known as 'administrative inertia'. It happens when emphasis is more on conformance to established norms rather than on innovation.

People are frustrated with slow, unresponsive public administrative systems that soak up large exchequer money in return for poor service.

Administrators resist change and control because they enjoy autonomy, they feel they know the best and they are their own masters. A citizen is often treated by an administrator as a subject and not as sovereign. Whenever a citizen comes in contact he is made to feel small by being made to wait or go around and around in circles in the name of rule, the concept of service or customer satisfaction is alien to the administrative culture. Administrator's attitude impedes the effective development of administration.

There is a general fallacy widely prevalent in the senior circles of bureaucracy that the top level administrators do not really need any kind of updating and that there is very little for them to learn.

Productivity of administrative system is low because not only it has accumulated too much fat but also due to:

- Unclear goals;
- Unclear accountability and responsibility;
- Rules dominating over value system and working culture;

- Unclear benchmark;
- Lack of exposure and awareness among those who work.

More so, the maladies of administrative apparatus are many:

- Tendency to regard itself as self-appointed;
- Redtape or undue formalism;
- Excessive departmentalisation, compartmentalisation;
- Unresponsiveness to justified demands of time and situation;
- Splitting of work into isolated and disintegrated activities;
- Subsections pursue their ends forgetting that they are only parts of the whole;
- Pro-conservatism and total aversion to change;
- Perpetual proneness to imposing prohibitions and restrictions.

Administrators too have their idiosyncracies and when they operate in conjunction with the administrative apparatus, it can be only awful, far away from the subtelities of the 'administrative value'. An administrator is:

- abominable 'no man'. Not a changer;
- nameless, faceless and soulless. Likes these attributes;
- formal, aloof, remote from realities of people, environment and social dynamics;
- precedent follower, sight is set to past not into the future;
- believes in hierarchy;
- power and status hungry;
- busy as much as he can in noting, drafting, redrafting, revising, rewriting etc.
- always in search of a scapegoat for his misdeeds and lacunae;

- a safe player, no enthusiasm, no dynamism, no trust;
- a believer in 'all credits are mine, all discredits theirs';
- lives in an insulated and quarantined world of his own;
- believes 'if no can be said, never say yes'.

Gerald E. Caiden has selected some meaningful words containing all these vices, maladies of administration what he calls *'bureaupathologies'*. In order to intensify the value content of administration these pathological symptoms are to be remedied.

Hardware aspects:

Main thrust for administrators should be: overallness, sense of horizontality, futuristic perception, productivity mindedness and systems approach.

Tomorrow is already expedited in today. Shift from 'position power' to 'relationship power' is already in force. Power and wealth will now rest on knowledge and information. The only empire that will survive in future will be the empire that you build in your mind. People of tomorrow will transmit knowledge and power.

Change and competition are unavoidable and it has started invading and winning through TQM, RE, ZOPP, Synergy, JIT etc. These concepts improve upon the value-content. TQM is total quality management in operation, maintenance and service, RE is Re-engineering is optimising the business process elements. ZOPP is acronym of German term Zieloientierte Projekt Planning which means objective oriented project planning. It is a tool to synthesise the experience, expertise and knowledge. Synergy means achieving a whole that is greater than its parts put together. JIT is supplying or serving 'just in time'.

Software Aspects:

Conceptually, productivity in administration envisages a result-oriented situation and not an activity oriented situation. In value-based administration productivity embraces efficiency as well as effectiveness with a bearing on quality in thought and action. There will be differing concern and importance for administration at different times. Administration which lacks value-based perspective will find difficulty in recognising and thus reacting to environmental changes.

While reflecting on value in administration, the interaction with the environment has to be kept in view. This may vary with:

(a) the efforts of administrator in meeting environmental requirements;

(b) changes in the environment that may be induced by administration;

(c) changes independently taking place in the environment.

Creativity in management may be either of the two:

- Non-surgical i.e. innovative, regenerative creative thinking, turn arounds;
- Surgical i.e. redesigning of practices, procedures, public policy, computerisation, discipline, modernisation, restructuring.

Replacement is better and less arduous than transformation Distance annihilation, information dissemination will be the routine daily activity. Rule and expenditure orientation will be replaced by mission and people orientation, result and productivity orientation. Delivering service will then be effective in terms of cost of service, quality of service and quantity of service.

Action Plan

(a) *Systemic change:* Hierarchy itself needs to be restructured. Number of people doing the same work need to be reduced. It may be achieved through:

  - overcoming rigidity;
  - adapt new techniques;
  - job enlargement for those at tedious positions;
  - promote competition.

(b) Commitment on priorities (comparative importance).

(c) *Import learning:* In Canada only telephones are used for any kind of horizontal memos/consultations, no paper work. In Russia any attempt to pass the buck is discouraged and matters involving high policy are considered by a collegium of officers.

(d) *Sound policying:* In policy making administrators must interact with other experts so that inputs (be it sociological, anthropological or otherwise) are available and the decision makers can gauge the decision situation in its total perspective and get the 'inner soul' realities.

(e) *Constant search:* There should be a constant search to find new ways to improve services to the people.

(f) *Questioning:* A public servant is to question himself as to:

- what exactly I am going to do?
- what harm may be caused by my action and to whom?
- is my action inevitable in the larger public interest?
- am I taking any steps to curb bad effects arising out of my decision?
- am I a time-server only or a quality-server?
- would my action stand against close public scrutiny?
- am I doing that to others what I would not have them do to me?

Epilogue

Political stability is directly relevant to administrator efficiency and economic productivity. Productivity will be poor where politics is the game of moral degenerates and administration is largely inhibited by self-seeking, mediocre bureaucrats indulging in abuse of power.

9

PSUs Then and Now

Fact not Fiction

Once upon a time people didn't like to work in PSUs (Public Sector Undertakings) although they were offering higher emoluments. They were considered as government companies only in which managers were not having actual powers but were bosses of an apparent power. The top brass of students preferred IAS, IFS and other allied services more than becoming PSU managers.

Then came a phase when young people were allured by the scale of pay offered by the PSUs. The IDA (Industrial Dearness Allowance), the work-culture of mistrust, disillusionment due to the skeleton in the cupboard etc. made the young managers quickly to form a beeline for private sector and MNC (Multi-National Companies) jobs—everyday the line is increasing. MNCs and private companies have also become hawkish and choosy in selecting PSU managers and meticulously eliminate those who have been only careerists at the cost of the company they served.

Most PSU corporate bodies smell of political flavour. Although the impression of a PSU corporate body appear as a 'team' but it is not so, it is only a 'conglomerate' of feuds and factions. There is sword-fighting, red-tapism even in petty matters of decision making. The work atmosphere, as such, is deteriorating very fast to a bottomless abyss. Who knows there may be much more uncertainty in store for PSU managers.

Contrary to the belief of those who are within and outside the PSU service it can be safely vouched that the PSUs today is on a downslide. It is due to two reasons: internal and external. Politicisation of PSUs, nepotism, various kinds of reservations have become a rider on the intake of quality professionals. Internally the decisions at corporate level are often politically driven; even promotions and inter/intra departmental shuffles often have ulterior motives. As a result sincerity, honesty, courage, performance are put in the dock.

Unless PSU managers have political bosses to back them hardly can be survive in the rat race of power. The power monger managers in PSUs believe that their power is supreme power, as it has no accountability. They also carry a wrong notion that they are to some extent immune to CBI or Vigilance inquiry. Thus goes the saga of a PSU manager. The intelligent PSU manager first searches for his political mentor based on caste relationships or from family standing to use such relation for his managerial prosperity.

Even if there is a courageous manager, none supports him, nor even the top management! In fact, all become spectators in an amphitheater watching the bloody fight of the courageous manager with the lion, ultimately succumbing to the powerful or winning, with irreparable personal losses.

The Exodus

Something drastically has gone wrong with PSU managers. They want to kick out their safe, insipid careers with PSUs and try their lucks with MNCs and good private concerns. They have been thinking, of late, why to break one's head in the labyrnthine, caste-ridden, false-performers and back at home with the wife; instead why not join an MNC and the wife is busy with the furnishing allowance, all the time she tries to figure out how to spend the amount.

The exodus has already started from banking, manufacturing, chimney-based factories, oil-extracting companies to MNCs. The cream is leaving the secured jobs of PSUs. All are running after comfort and recognition. The exodus is due to the wide hiatus between the reality and the PSU manager's expectations. They want good infrastructure-based, flexible, learning organisations with healthy inter-personal relations up and across the hierarchies. Nobody wants to be an insignificant high-performing employee because the credit of his fruits of labour goes to somebody else.

The Malaise

Often in PSUs, any single lapse on the part of a senior executive is condemned through man-made punishments so that the career paths of other mediocres are not obstructed. In PSUs the sincere fellow, the honest fellow, the punctual fellow are good for nothing. He who shows his face to the boss at the 'beginning of work' and at the 'end of work' becomes the blue-eyed boy. Many PSU managers do not work throughout the year but they ensure showing their face daily to the boss during January to March for the CCR is written next month.

Such managers even do not mind to be with the boss till late night only to keep their CCR in tact. Interestingly when the boss is transferred to another section and no longer remains the boss the manager who was subordinate yesterday avoids to even inquire about the well being of the ex-boss. Everything is allowed in this game of man and his boss!

This is the reason why in PSUs the bosses are flying birds, the managers do not own their company. Everybody wants to pass his time, as a time server only not as a contributor or a reformer. Industrial service in PSU is not 'work management' but 'boss management', at any cost.

Of course, all PSUs are not the same from perk point of view. Everything depends on financial condition, the quality of manpower they have and the attitude of the decision maker i.e. the CEO (Chief Executive Officer). A number of PSUs have attractive fascade: good looking offices, receptionists, modern partition walls, glass sheets everywhere but the people working have low morale, low satisfaction. A balance has not so far been maintained between the fascade and the people, the hardware and the software part.

Factors which have added to the poor performance of the PSUs are many, but to name a few:

Internal factors:

- culture of complacence;
- excessive hierarchy;
- non co-operation among departments;
- inadequate role clarity and accountability;
- inadequate appreciation for genuine good work;
- more work heroes less work horses;
- encouragement of dark horses at the time of promotion;
- culture of convenience;
- absence of long term orientation;
- frequent replacement of top management by worse successors;
- lack of trust;
- desire for status quo;
- lack of initiative arising out of unsuccessful past attempts;
- dislike of management's discretion and biases;
- highly bureaucratic practices;
- translucent organisations.

External factors:

- political interference in major decision making;
- top management posts are political and their change politically motivated;
- more inclination towards political masters than corporate experts;

- inadequate coordination with vital agencies;
- constraints in inputs;
- health of existing assets dependent on availability of spares, monopoly market.

Most of the young managers feel recognition of creativity, creative work and the creative men etc. never define the philosophy of PSUs, except of course, a few stray coverage in PR bulletins just to indicate that yes the eye of management also looks at all these. In house talents, if any, are considered as obstacles against routine work. In other words, creativity retards the growth vis-a-vis routine activity.

PSUs must remember that not all changes lead to progress, and all progress is change. Undertakings have expertise, but knowledge without integrity has often caused wickedness because only knowledge with integrity is wisdom. Due to this, must PSU managers did not enjoy life at every given point, work done by him is not what he likes to do. Most of his efforts are directed never to do anything wrong. Often the work done by him in distasteful manner never resulted in anything good.

Productivity depends on a full-stomach. This stands true for both blue as well as white collar jobs. But overloading reduces it drastically.

Health clubs, family holidays, overseas trips, laptop PCs are only confined to the top brass of PSU managers, that is too a limited few. Five-star comfort, AC comfort in railways, magazine and entertainment allowance, newspapers in offices vanish on a fine morning as a part of cost-control measures in PSUs but the fittest thrive on kickbacks through quarterly planning of spares, scarp auction, imports, compromising with quality to save so called cost etc.

What most of the PSUs do not have are: good physical environment, old PCs (personal computers) waiting for years to be upgraded for want of formal procedure, non-toxic bosses etc. More available in PSUs are highly toxic bosses, non-working bosses, gospel-preaching bosses, obsolete communication systems, dilapidated office furniture and appliances, poor exposure and close mentality of middle and top managers. So the young managers find with whom to grow, upon whom to lean upon!

Penny wise pound foolish attitude is not uncommon towards training and development. Whenever there is cost control the sword falls on training—all outdoor training is stopped abruptly. Certain routine activities instead are conducted with snacks/lunch. As a result it is not at all 'effective'. The basic purpose of outdoor training is to move outside the operations area and get a bird's eye-view of the situation. This enables to know whether what one is doing is right thing. A different and unexpected environment not only helps creativity to flow but also improves acceptability of each other, team spirit grows.

Training and development requires a turn around. Only skill, technical development, refresher, statutory modules are not enough. Interestingly, 85 per cent of the jobs obtained or promotions received are based on attitude and the remaining 15 per cent on education and skill. Attitude development is slow but is catching up very fast. Motorola Company claims that for every dollar invested in human resources the return is 30 dollars.

Measures

Let there be a fresh 'concourse'. A concourse is a gathering of people, at a common place, for a common purpose, for creating an honest, sincere, genuine, down-to-earth atmosphere, with a fiery unconventionalism and soothing innovativeness.

PSUs must remember that not all changes lead to progress and not all progress is change. Undertakings have expertise, but knowledge without integrity has often caused wickedness because only knowledge with integrity is wisdom. Due to this most PSU managers do not enjoy life at every given point. Work done by him is not what he likes to do. Most of his efforts are directed never to do anything wrong. Often the work done by him in distasteful manner never resulted in anything good.

There is a global shift in management is from 'control' to 'support'. Monetary reward is not sufficient, showing appreciation is also the requirement of today for any good work.

Unless PSU managers are picked up forcibly for compulsory exposure to PCs, software, modern PC languages and the whole manpower must be identified as 'servitors' and 'survivors'. Servitors should limit themselves to routine traditional work patterns whereas survivors are to be developed more and more to manage the future positions.

In PSU managers are 'yes' men. They do not want to hurt the bosses. But when they fail or pass the problem elsewhere, sweet nothing excuses are given to the boss. So for all PSU bosses, if any manager says 'yes, I can do it' or 'sir, I cannot do this' should be taken critically. May be both are actually meaning the same. Under such circumstances either the individual does not know how to it therefore requires technical/special training or he does not want to do it hence requires attitudinal training.

In order to make a PSU or any business a success one can take a few tips from Shiv Khera's thoughts. He says:

- Don't do different things, learn to do things differently;
- Success without fulfilment is empty;
- People do most for a belief;
- People do things for their reasons and not yours;
- Systems won't work if people don't;
- Bigger the problem, bigger the opportunity.

In Indian management scenario technology ceases to be the cutting edge of competition. If people don't work what the system can do? What is required is a change in attitude. Organisations must realise that their most valuable resources is their people and in turn the employees' attitude. Ironically, this resource is most neglected.

Challenges for the PSUs are their own weaknesses viz.

- lack of team work;
- redefinition roles absent;
- restructuring of organisations missing;
- absence of decentralisation of decision making;

- poor communication down the line;
- lack of criticism against poor work-culture;
- mismanagement of interface with govt.;
- lack of respect for authority;
- lack of commitment from top management;
- employees involvement inadequate;
- inactivity of trade unions except for their own interest;
- middle management not owning responsibility;
- dedicated employees kept on toes but not others;
- loyal customers in market non-existent;
- inadequate exposure to competitive environment;
- absence of proactivity;
- adopting bureaucratic methods from govt.;
- lack of concern about people.

10

Essentials of Drucker

Prophylaxix for PSUs

On Business

Business is a process which converts a resource, distinct knowledge, into a contribution of economic value in the market place. Peter Drucker told way back in 1954 in the Practice of Business that the purpose of business is to create a customer.

Interestingly

1. Neither results nor resources exist inside business. In fact business can be defined as a process that converts an outside resource, namely knowledge, into outside results, namely economic values.
2. Results are obtained by exploiting opportunities only.
3. Resources, in order to produce results must b e allocated to opportunities rather than problems.
4. Economic results are earned only by leadership not by mere competence.
5. Any leadership position is transitory and likely to be shortlived. This is based on Schumpeter's theorem that

profits result only from the innovator's advantage and therefore disappear as soon as the innovation has become routine.

6. What exists is getting old. What exists therefore is always aging. Any human decision or action, however courageous or appropriate, it may be, starts to get old the moment it has been made.

7. What exists is likely to be misallocated. Unless management constantly works at directing efforts into 'revenue-producing' activities, the costs will tend to allocate themselves by drifting into 'nothing-producing' activities.

8. Concentration is the key to economic results. HR must be concentrated on major opportunities which are very few. Concentration on 'these few activities' gives significant business results.

Business enterprise is not a phenomenon of nature but one of society. There are three dimensions to the *economic task* behind any business:

- *The present business must be made effective;*
- *Its potential must be identified and realised;*
- *It must be made into a different business for a different future.*

The idea of business sums up answers to questions:

- What is our business?
- What should it be?
- What will it have to be?

Executives

Executives are the monarchs and manipulators of the 'present'; they give neither sufficient time nor sufficient thought to the 'future'. This is a neglect. They and their business may have to pay a penalty. In fact today's job takes away all the executive's time, although the job may not be done well. *Many managers are elated about their immediate task only.*

Future

But tomorrow always arrives—as new and different. If one has not worked on the future, trouble shall lurk over. Only remaining a slothful steward of the talents given in his keeping is not enough, the executive has to accept responsibility for making the future happen. He is to be a business builder rather than the executive-suite custodian.

The hard realities of the present must not be obscured by the lure of tomorrow's promises. The difficult and risky work for tomorrow must not be smothered by the urgencies of the present.

Making the Future Today

Two things that are certain about the future are:

1. It cannot be known.
2. It will be different from what exists now and from what we expect.

Therefore,

- Any attempt to base today's actions and commitment or predictions of future events is futile;
- The best is to anticipate future effects of events which have already irrevocably happened;
- To try to make the future happen is risky but it is a rational activity;
- Risk is better than coasting along on the comfortable assumption that nothing is going to happen or change.

Making the future is not to decide what should be done tomorrow, but what should be done today to have a tomorrow. Entrepreneur is a related word coined by J.B. Say, French economist in 1800 AD which describes a man who attracts capital locked up in the unproductive past and commits it to the risk of making a different future.

Disagreements

Disagreements are important. They bring out searching questions about company, its products, policies, direction etc. Often the questioners may misinterpret what they experience but none the less the experience as such is real and relevant.

Disagreements need not be concealed or explained away. "Right questions" are more valuable than "right answers". Decision through acclamation is more dangerous than decision through questions of importance.

Idea

An idea has power. It need not be a big idea but it must be one that differs from the norm of today. It is not certain that the more imaginative ideas will be more successful. Pedestrian ideas have at times been successful. There are many ideas in organisations but are hardly put to use. What matters is courage rather than genius.

What is lacking is 'looking beyond products to ideas'. Products are processes are only the vehicle through which an idea becomes effective. The test of an idea is its economic performance and economic result not acclaim or praise by philosophers.

Idea must meet the test of personal commitment. Do we really believe in the idea? *If the idea is not both 'uncertain' and 'risky' it is not a practical idea for the future. For the future itself is both uncertain and risky. Future cannot be made on those riskless ideas that cannot fail.* To make the future demands real courage, work and faith.

Posteriorities

Priority decisions bespeak the level of a management's vision and seriousness. They decide basic behaviour and strategy. Nobody seems to have difficulty in setting priorities but in setting 'posteriorities' i.e. on what should not be done.

Knowledge

Knowledge is specifically human resource. It is not found in books. Books contain only information; whereas knowledge is the ability to apply information to specific work and performance. They comes with a human being only, his brain or the skill of his hands.

Many managers are knowledgeable (having knowledge without utility) but for business success, knowledge must first be meaningful to the customer in terms of satisfaction and value.

Knowledge realities are:

- A valid definition of specific knowledge of a business sounds simple but deceptively so.
- It takes practice to do knowledge analysis well. Management must ask objective, searching and productive questions to itself: What is our specific knowledge?
- Knowledge is a perishable commodity. It has to be reaffirmed, re-learned and repractised all the time. One has to work constantly at regaining one's specific excellence but how can one maintain one's excellence unless one knows what it is.
- Every knowledge eventually becomes the wrong knowledge. It becomes obsolete. Perennial questions often come up: What else do we need? Do we need something different?
- No company can excel in many knowledge areas. Most business remain marginal and just manage to hang on.

Knowledge Analysis

A successful business has to be competent in good many areas in addition to being excellent in one. Knowledge analysis is necessary and is to be fed to market analysis and conclusions of market analysis to be projected to the knowledge analysis to bring out needs for new or changed knowledge. Knowledge analysis leads to certain diagnostic questions like:

1. Do we have the right knowledge? Knowledge has to progress to remain knowledge. Knowledge is like an athletic record which stands apparently immovable for years. One man breaks the record of excellence by jumping a little higher or running a little faster. What one man has done, another can always do again. This is particularly true with respect to excellence.

2. Are we actually getting paid for the knowledge we contribute?
3. Is our knowledge sufficiently built into our goods and services?
4. How can we improve? What are we missing? And how do we go about supplying it?

Risks and Opportunities

Business must try to minimise risks. Minimising risk does not mean no risk. Any attempt to escape risk may ultimately land in the risk of doing nothing.

There are four kinds of risk:

1. The risk one must accept, the risk that is built into the very nature of business;
2. The risk one can afford to take;
3. The risk one cannot afford to take;
4. The risk one cannot afford not to take.

1 is necessary to say in the business. 2 is imminent when it is a matter of losing money or effort invested. If one is unable to exploit the success which may arise then one falls back on 3. Whenever there is breakthrough opportunity there is risk of 4th kind: a risk one cannot afford not to take.

Any action must not only minimise risk but also maximise opportunities. There are three kinds of opportunities:

- *Additive:* It exploits fully the existing resources. It does not change character of business;
- *Complementary:* If offers something new, when combined with the existing, results in a new total larger than its parts. It is synergesic. It changes the structure of business.
- *Breakthrough:* It requires great effort. It changes fundamental economic characteristics and capacity of business.

Interestingly an opportunity which runs 'counter' to the 'idea' of business may be the 'right' opportunity. Such incongruence between the basic idea of business and a major opportunity may be the first indication that a 'redefinition' of the very idea of business is necessary.

Specialisation, Diversification and Integration (SDI)

Every business needs a core, an area where it leads. Every business must therefore specialise(S). Every business must also obtain the most from specialisation, that is, it must diversify (D). Balance between the two i.e. S and D defines the scope of business and largely determine the productivity of a company. In isolation each of these is seldom productive.

Business also needs integration(I) otherwise business soon cease to speak a common language. Integration is often used as a means to diversify or to concentrate. Forward integration i.e. extension of the business scope toward the market adds diversification. Backward integration i.e. integration from the market to manufacturing or from manufacturing to the raw materials is often a way to concentrate.

SDI are strategies of high impact but also of high risk. They should be subjected to two kinds of tests:

1. The test of economic results.
2. The test of economic risk.

Structure and Strategy

Chandler demonstrates that structures follows strategy and Miss Penrose makes it clear that growth demands the right structure. Right structure does not guarantee results but the wrong structure aborts results and smothers even the best directed efforts.

No matter how well suited to the needs of today's business, organisations must be reviewed as the business changes.

11

Prevention of Corrupt Practices in PSUs

Prelude

Under Part-IV of the Constitution of India, one of the directives is: "the state shall strive to promote the welfare of the people by serving and protecting as effectively as it may a social order in which justice, social, economic and political shall inform all the institutions of the national life". It also envisages to minimise inequalities in income, status facilities and opportunities among individuals and groups of people residing in different areas or engaged in different vocations. With the formations of the public sectors like railways, mining, power, steel etc. the economy has been in the public hands.

Although the structure of our democratic republic is based on the hard and durable foundation of socialism, unfortunately the view of people about the system has been adverse. They say the administration machinery or the management is not only slow moving and inefficient but corrupt. To make such a machinery move there have been experiences narrated as to how somebody's palm is to be greased, how an influential person is to put a word or how speed money is paid to get the routine work done and also for getting legitimate claims like a telephone connection, gas connection, railway reservation. Today corruption covers areas like recruitment, service confirmation, promotion, transfer, felicitation, quarter allotment, sanction of loans and advances, licence, permits etc. The middle-man or the hench-man thrive on all these. Hardly anyone says his work was done without harassment and/or without anybody's assistance.

Most of us believe in superficiality. We scratch the crust and say that earth is nothing but soil and stones and a few minerals. Those who go deep enough might find water underneath and deeper one goes hotter it is and everything is in liquid form. To find out the liquidity of corruption, we may have to go to the depths that determine human behaviour. The viscera of corruption is as follows:

— Corruption starts in a small way among some people only;

— Corruption keeps on increasing till it is deep-rooted, widespread and incurable;

— Corruption develops immunity sand even resists easy detection or cure;

— Corruption spreads till novel methods are invented to raise rates and levels;

— Corruption generates commission agents to cover actual bribe-takers and to encourage free market of corruption.

Kautilya had no good opinion on the financial integrity of individuals and in his Arthashastra has indicated metaphorically in Book 2, Sutras 33 and 34 respectively:

- Just as fish moving inside water cannot be known when drinking water even so officers appointed carrying out work cannot be known when appropriating money.
- It is possible to know even the path of the birds flying in the sky but not the ways of the officers moving with their intentions concealed.

1997 World Bank Report describes corruption as 'abuse of public power for private gain'. Oxford dictionary defines corruption as (a) corrupt morals, behaviour etc.; (b) dishonest especially through accepting bribes. The former sense is used when spoken of corruption of young people; the latter sense is used in senior bureaucratic people. Corruption is a cognizable offence under the Provision of Prevention of Corruption Act 1988 Section 7, 8, 9, 11 and 13 against the misconduct committed by a public servant involved in:

— Bribery or illegal gratification;

— Amassing amounts disproportionate to known sources of income;

— Misappropriation, embezzlement and defalcation;

— Fraud and forgery;

— Abuse of authority.

A Perception of PSUs

PSUs are located in different states with varied backdrop of cultures and systems. In most cases the production costs are mounting higher and productivity is low, one of the many reasons maybe possibly due to poor and dishonest management. Corruption was confined to few people at lower levels in a very few departments. Today it has spread to practically all levels of most departments. Owing to this prices have to be raised every now and then to make up the losses, yet losses go on mounting due to unchecked malpractices and corruption. It is almost like storing water in a leaking vessel.

One hears of substandard stores being purchased or good items of inventory being clandestinely sold as scrapes to make illegal personal gain. Huge quantities of unwanted stores are purchased and later allowed to be pilfered or wasted. At the points/posts of inspection, assessment and collection of material or revenue as the case may be, the post holders get away with substantial personal gain. Hospitals suffer from lack of essential medicine, ghost paper purchases are often talked. Transport system and heavy mining machinery are burdened with high operation and maintenance costs may be due to bogus purchase of spares, oil, lubricants etc.

Corrupt persons complain against the honest ones who come in their way and honest persons feel jealous of the illicit acquisitions of the corrupt, thus completing the cycle of mutual complaint. There are 'big egos and small men' and 'small men and big ego. It is time to apply reverse gear to stop further deterioration of administrative standards, integrity and values.

Root Causes of Fall

Power corrupts and absolute power corrupts absolutely. Perception in previous paragraph can be analysed from SPM point of view. SPM stands for Service, Power and Money. This SPM syndrome varies in degree for different individual position. Service offers complete satisfaction and delight, it is slow but produces lasting effect. Power is the quickest in yielding results. Money is the most startling in motivation. Service is operational ideal, caring instinct. Between Power and Money the former does not come into play unless one tastes it; but the latter is possessive, magnetic and one forgets every kind of affinity, blood relationship when it comes to acquisition or parting of money. Money has been prolific source of corrupt practices. Service, power and money produce different patterns of relationship (between their users and those who are at the receiving end).

In PSUs there are multidimensional crises like: crisis of character, crisis of leadership, crisis of focussing, crisis of bureaucracy, crisis of motivation, crisis of vision, crisis of implementation. There are numerous causes for this fall in standards of integrity and efficiency:

— Social climate has been highly materialistic;

— Rat race in the hierarchies is rampant instead of healthy competition;

— No scruples or ethics in rat race in elbowing one's way ahead;

— Money making is considered fair;

— Emphasis is on 'making' money than 'earning' money;

— Vulgar display of personal assets in both residence and in office;

— Illicit acquisitions considered as status symbol.

Temptation for corruption is aggravated due to inadequate remuneration or delay in pay and related perquisites. Often the salary and perks do not match with the price index or inflation. Many succumb to make extra money whenever and wherever there is opportunity. Unfortunately such people are made to occupy high positions and promotions are accelerated without any check even to the chagrin of the plethora of witnessing people. On the contrary, innocents for their unintentional and trivial lapses are cautioned, reprimanded and even punished just to exercise the provisions of the CDA rules. Such prejudicial actions unfortunately encourages corruption and throttles the spirit of honesty and good work.

Often the concept of godfather is in use in the PSUs. Persons of high power and influence inside or outside the PSU units shield and protect the corrupt and the inefficient ensuring their quick riser in the hierarchies of management. Undesirable pulls and pressures are exercised in the matters of posting, promotions, and transfers etc. disturbing the internal chain of command and control. Due to dubious conduct of the positions of power, who are instrumental in such unjust treatment, there is hardly any fear of higher ups which ultimately has culminated into mismanagement.

In most of the PSUs there is a strong feeling has developed that good work hardly gets rewarded and bad conduct seldom gets punished if there is some godfather to protect.

Preventive Measures

Unless corruption and malpractices are checked it will retard the economic and also the social progress of the people serving any PSUs. Unless prevented, there will be a situation where only might will be right and reverting to the law of the jungle making life short, nasty and brutish. Urgent corrective measures are to be taken to make the apparatus of administration efficient and clean so that there is no burden on the people. It can be done through preventive, detective and punitive methods. Some of these can be listed as follows:

- Reducing areas of discretion;
- Reducing areas of patronage;

- Simplification of rules and procedures;
- Deregulation in identified areas of corruption;
- Rewarding and promoting those who are efficient and above any suspicion;
- Abnormal efficiency in susceptible areas of corruption to examined;
- Closer watch on officials of doubtful integrity;
- Verification of movable/immovables of officials of doubtful integrity;
- Inquiry and deterrent punishment of proven cases, wide publicity of punishment;
- Weeding out the corrupt through premature retirement;
- Identifying areas blocking and delaying;
- Identifying areas/departments where there is decrease in discipline;
- Unnecessary and duplication of work to be curtailed;
- Ill gotten wealth, if any, should be confiscated fully after full inquiry.

Preventive vigilance through awareness workshops can be taken up. Silent hard working officials must be rewarded. It must be remembered that anonymity is the best virtue of a truly honest and efficient official. Long tenures in a post and/or place often breeds corruption. Once vision and plan are clear the occupants of various posts can be mobile at shorter intervals. Greater check at corruption prone areas/activities is required. Identification of hard core corrupt elements and discovering the hidden channels of bribe are challenging tasks.

When individuals are in collision course and there are mud slinging, then corruption may be hidden, may be personal interest is adversely affected. Any kind of vigilant agency should not be a watchdog only, they should be proactive keeping track of developments at human interaction level instead of reactive.

The general reputation and record of service to be taken due note of before anybody is reprimanded. Anonymous letters/ complaints where complainant does not disclose identity only imply that there can't be smoke unless there is fire somewhere and such complaints may be ignored after preliminary verification if deemed fit. Effective vigilance requires existence of an effective chain of command to enforce discipline and good conduct. Effective chain of command is possible, if there is an in-built arrangement to reward good work and punish misconduct without any outside interference, pull or pressure.

Purposeful social opinion will create the right environment for an organisation to function. Media and other channels like CCTV, workshops, communiques, dos and don'ts booklets, social plays etc. can be used to mould public perception and opinion in the desired direction. Ostracism and social sanction would be much better when we are attempting large-scale holistic transformation like prevention of corrupt practices.

Epilogue

However in spite of this prevailing gloom, fortunate for PSUs that there are still a large number of people at all levels and ion all departments who still perform their duties with sincerity, dedication and honesty. In spite of general decline of value their conduct remains beyond reproach and they only provide hope and light in the dark arena. The vigilance machinery, the vigilance commission, the management should take adequate care so that such persons do not fall victim to their ignorance, as to err is human. Any stigma on any honest person shall not only shake the morale irreparably but make the system and procedure a laughing stock.

The vital points which require critical appreciation and vigilant analysis are:

— False allegation;

— False and motivated complaints;

— Arbitrary action;

— Leniency towards trivial/ignorant omissions;

— Harassment by groups/interested parties;

— Personal grudge by superiors and victimisation of subordinates;

— Pseudo-integrity of self-controlling officials/chosen guardians;

— Misuse of power by holders of power.

Continuous and critical review of decisions taken by those CEOs whose dossier files have been opened by CBI, IB, CVC etc. So that it becomes an eye-opener to the successors and they exercise the delegated power gracefully. Administrative anger need not poison the apparatus of the system.

Whenever there is silence especially when the good people remain silent, it must be taken with a pinch of salt, because when something goes wrong, injustice is to be levied there is a lull. New strategy and chain of command to be introduced at select vital areas under close monitoring. It may be pretty difficult to bring an order or inculcate any value in large PSU workforce. Catching and punishing here and there won't be effective at all. What is required is internal discipline through proper delegation of authority and power at appropriate levels.

It must be remembered that:

- Any sort of work must have a sense of fear, sincerity and responsibility;
- Any work with a sense of mission, sacrifice and result orientation must be admired;
- Honesty and ability to decide between the right and wrong are qualities as important as any professional competence;
- Continuous Rethinking Reinventing refines any system.

A public servant is expected to be role model of social and familial behaviour of society. He shall maintain absolute integrity, he should be politically neutral and should be impartial and non-corrupt.

12

Management
Not That Easy

The Open Secret

Thomas Teal in the Harvard Business Review (Oct-Nov' 96) says refreshingly the management is complex because we focus too much on technical efficiency and too little on character. We forget the fact that after all managing is not a mere series of mechanical, impersonal tasks but a meaningful set of highly human interactions. Teal says: "The best managers I have seen serve two masters: organisation and moral". The secret of best management means:

- Being responsible for one's people;
- Being able to clearly communicate with them;
- Keeping one's promise or commitment;
- Knowing first one's own limitations;
- Trying to do better everyday;
- Remembering that human beings are selfish first, other matters come next;
- Acting on basics: A smile and a pat means the same in any language.

Today good management means scientific management, rationalised production, democratised wealth, science commercialised reaching common man and effectively doubling life expectancy etc. All these mean progressing ahead of where we were in pre-scientific management period.

The Surgical Opening

A close look at any company in trouble helps in locating the major problems in its management. Very often management itself is the biggest barrier to creativity, innovation, change, new ideas etc. Also, when opportunities are missed or projects are bungled up the ultimate responsibility lies with the management. When practised by others management appears to be easy for the peers, but it is not that easy as it appears to be.

Rise of mediocrity is natural. Managements too may be mediocre; this is not because wrong people are promoted or the system manipulated but because capable management is not that easy to achieve. That is why most managers often complain about trying their very best and their inability to achieve the expected level. Such things happen due to a common job making uncommon demand on the manager.

A surgical opening of the manager reveals that he has to acquire considerable functional expertise in traditional areas like finance, cost control, manufacturing, processing, fund allocation, marketing, technology, HRD and other functional areas. The same manager is also required to master management art and craft: strategy, persuasion, speaking, listening, negotiation; to demonstrate qualities that define leadership, integrity, character; we expect him to possess vision, fortitude, intelligence, insight, commitment, passion, sensitivity, sensibility, ethical, standards, charisma, courage, humility, tenacity and what not! We further insist the managers to be sociable, good guardians, friends and mentors as per the roles he has been hemmed into. Practising the management as a profession means combining all these extreme skills and displaying. Many managers do feel to have under-performed while meeting these extremes expected of him.

Paradigm Shift

In India and abroad managers talk about Lean and Mean; to have lean set up (slim, nonfatty organisational structure) and to have mean measures (cost-effective business). These two are necessary because there is a competitive edge to win over in order to survive. Who bothers to remember the names of the losers these days? Getting a competitive edge is the order of the day. Peter F. Drucker has said in the HBR (May-June' 93): "...changing an organisation from 'flow of things' to 'flow of information' where concepts of 'rank' and 'power' have to be replaced by 'mutual understanding' and 'responsibility'...". There is a clear paradigm shift in the trend of management philosophy.

Characteristics	**Old Nomenclature**	**New Philosophy**
Strategy	Planned	Entrepreneurial
Structure	Hierarchy	Network
Systems	Rigid	Flexible
Staff	Imposing	Co-operative
Skills	To complete	To build
Style	Problem solving	Transformation
Shared values	Sameness	Meaningful differences
Sources of strength	Stability	Change
Leadership	Dogmatic	Inspirational
Focus	Institutional	Individual/Team
Roles	Fragmented	Integrated
Ethos	Self-centered	Value based
Orientation	Rule oriented	Ethical oriented

Old motivations are no longer motivating enough. Business manager must develop brand new ways to encourage performance and build commitment. Attractive remuneration is not enough, the firms need to concentrate on what young managers want and cherish. Loyalty is no longer a bond between a person and the company; rather the new loyalty is only a weak link now. Attachment to one's own profession/discipline has become stronger than ever before. Any team-building requires to keep in view this aspect.

Ms. Rosabeth Kanter gives five words which may attract young managers to stick and not to quit any organisation.

Mission: Good leaders give a missionary vision. The pride in respective work is the better motivation than promotion-based reward system.

Control of the Agenda: Career paths and company future have their own uncertainty. Managers leave glamorous jobs in favour of jobs which give freedom and self control on their own activities.

Learning: Organisation and its members in continual learning matters. Absence of learning indicates degeneration and stagnation for the young.

Reputation: Is the key inspiration in an professional career. Chance to enhance it adds to motivation projecting a better self-image.

Share of Value-creation: Extra rewards or entrepreneurial incentive or team actions based on measurable results do attract. Consuming resources only is no longer viewed creative activity.

In old model top executive was to figure out what was going on, to make key decisions and create control mechanisms that would translate top management's decisions into co-ordinated actions throughout the organisation i.e. Planning Organising and Controlling (POC): the trinity of traditional authoritarian management. But, today, this is rapidly changing. It is no longer easy to figure out everything at the top. Top management's insights and decisions become obsolete by the time they reach front ranks. As such, people down the line don't have any tendency to pay attention to such matters anyway!

Business Creativity

We are in an age of business creativity. Information technology has ushered this new creative era. Management is transforming its role from controller to emancipator of creativity. This is the latest managerial mind-set. Business, creativity is nothing but a knife that grows sharper in the hands of astute business oriented manager. Mere access to information does not automatically bestow power. The new trinity today is: Information, Intelligence and Creativity. Intelligence is the ability to hold two contradictory ideas in the head at the same time. Contradiction and divergence create puzzle, tension and stress. Encompassing contradiction and the instrinctive desire to overcome the divergence can be achieved only with creativity.

A manager who picks up faster, in a deft manner to fill up gap, to resolve conflict, forging inter-relationship, conducting hidden relations etc. is a creative player. Creative management of various cross currents, whether it is man-management, process management, market retailing or whatever, determine the winners and losers.

How many practitioners of management understand the depth of commitment required to build a learning organisation? First of all, to be a real learner is to be ignorant and incompetent. How many top executives will care to declare that? Edgar Schein says most top executives have little understanding of the task of developing culture. It requires Patience, Reflectiveness and above all a Willingness to find a "new balance" between:

- Focussing on results; and
- Focussing on how we are operating while we are trying to achieve those results.

Learning organisations represent a "fundamental shift" in organisational culture. This fundamental shift is inevitable sooner or later in all organisations because the managers are already going through a profound change in the nature of their managerial work.

Preparing for Epochal Change

Drucker's thoughts, Parkinson's law, Peter Principle are undoubtedly useful as they contain words of wisdom which are practical. However, serious management study means much more. Today it is more necessary to manage change than controlling the company. Time pressured and boss-terrorised managers are many and they are the persons who try to remain constant, oblivious of the change. We are approaching a change-point in the tide of time. Last 500 years of societal metamorphosis is closing and thereby implying another epochal change unfolding itself. May, be in the lexicon of 2000-2500 AD 'self' will be the first entry and 'loyalty' relegated to the archaic category!

There is an urgent need for business leaders to 'reposition' themselves and 'rethink' competition strategies. For survival in the coming times American business men are going for activities like 'stop planning', 'forget process', 'practice intelligent disobedience' 'listen to your own life', 'build unrules into the structures', 'surrender control' etc. But before initiating we in India should examine their credibility. Possible what India needs is a living business strategy for sustainability matching with the changing circumstances.

13

My View on the Philosophy of Human Resource Development

If all of us remember, at the earliest input of education of our life, caring for human beings was taught to us and we learnt it well. This small lesson is very much within us, but deeply buried, under the mammoth load of sedimentations of worklife, aspirations, grievances, stakes, targets etc. The need of the time now is to go to basics.

Certain fundamental questions are to be asked, in order to introspect ourselves:

In our living life, in general:

- Are we treating ourselves with respect?
- Are we treating the other human beings while attributing animal qualities or pristine human qualities which are next to divine?
- What causes human beings to brim with qualities of caring and sharing?
- Can I transform to transcend by limitations, and do the same for the other?

- Am I a complete and wholesome human being upholding human emotions and values?

In the limited sphere of organisation, in particular:

- Are we planning for other's self-development, other's competency?
- What causes to compromise with one's lifetime core values and even allow their violation? Is it worthwhile?
- How and by whom the human dignity is threatened?
- What effect I am making to improve organisational culture?
- Am I instrumental in any transformational action meant for employee?

These questions are only illustrative and can be framed as per requirement. The word 'development' occurring in the HRD means 'what is desirable'. In human dimensions it has two edges:

- While praising tell the employees in clear terms, what was done was right. Tell how people feel about it. Shake hands and/or touch people while praising, after all they are fellow humans.
- Reprimand people immediately and tell clearly what they did was wrong and tell what others felt about it. Discourage to repeat.

In essence, HRD is not merely limited to a 'label' of the times; nor it is a sophisticated gospel preached by a few and understood by very few but a continuous creativity, renewing all the time a proactive human environment. It is a developmental step, in the process of evolution covering all homo-sapiens to transcend himself; in the interest of mankind.

14

Develop or Die

A New Leaf of Thought on HRD as a Profession

Introduction

If all of us remember, as the earliest input of education, caring for human beings was taught to us and we learnt it well. This small lesson is very much within us, but deeply buried under the mammoth load of sediments of work-life, aspirations, grievances, stakes.

Every advancement begins in a small way and with the individual. Man is a technological animal, thus he is sometimes called homo faber, man the maker. Only man has evolved culturally to the point where he only can alter consciously and radically his physical environment and his own biological make up. Biological process is not analytical but are 'wholes'; they are different from the sum of their parts. Information is indeed conceptual but meaning is not, it is perception. Knowledge therefore, becomes the real capital of the developed economy. Learning is coping and coping is survival.

It is people who make things happen and bring changes. People need to be developed to initiate change, participate in it, facilitate it and manage it in the desired direction. People understand and participate in change and precisely for this reason, unless there is professionalism, sometimes they become beneficiaries or victims.

Features of Development

Development involved unfolding of structure over time, encompassing ever more complex levels of organisation. Business is no longer directed by individual intelligence but by intelligences interacting and ceaselessly influencing one another.

Development of all kinds conforms to a series of laws, which are true equally of a living organism and a business. Some of the futures are:

- Development occurs in time in series of stages;
- Development is principally discontinuous;
- Within each stage a particular structure in development tends to dominate;
- A shift occurs to a new pattern of relationship;
- Development is irreversible;
- Development is qualitative;
- It is dynamically balanced;
- It is interspersed with evolutionary crises.

Any kind of development mostly has a longer calm period of growth described as 'evolutionary' which ends after a characteristic period, in crisis and turmoil termed 'revolutionary'. A major solution in one time period may become a major problem at a future date. As such in HRD instead of any isolated solution a relational solution is suggested.

Need of a Profession

Man is not only a mass of flesh, bone, blood, water conglomerate; nor should he be treated as a machine or an element of production process. A great plasticity is rather needed to deal with the beings' complex motives. Should man be a commodity which will be kept motivated only through payment? Must technological advancement swell man's ego and shrink his conscience?

After all, managing is not a mere series of mechanical, impersonal tasks but a meaningful set of highly human interactions. Unless human beings are developed by professionally sound methods to the desired level no effort of management can be meaningful. Knowing the other person's self is of crucial significance. P & L is profit and loss at primal economic but also can be people and love at human developmental level.

Dissatisfaction with the status quo is a fundamental trait of the human race. This trait is responsible for all human development. Since development is inevitable, it is rational to think of a profession called HRD. Unless man is professionally guided to control the rate of change in his personal affairs as well as society around him, he is domed to a massive adaptational breakdown.

HRD as a profession is a new coinage but it has roots in traditional wisdom. This professional is a kind of a missionary:

- Most people act in order to fulfill their desires and they believe that the world serves them but the missionary serves others and is relatively desireless, even defenceless;
- Most people lead busy lives but the missionary is quiet and reflective whenever at leisure;
- Most people seek stimulation and novelty but the missionary prefers what is common and natural.

HRD as a Profession

Man lives in several planes at once and his development depends on uniting them. Reconciliation of personal freedom and the constitutional order is the key; developmental manager is the master of these three which a non-professional won't dare to use.

The shift of the concept of personnel management to HRD is the first step in adopting a larger perspective. The inherent preference of organisation is clarity, certainty and perfection. The inherent nature of human relation is ambiguity, uncertainty and imperfection. The real management is balancing and integrating.

Peter Senge says in his book The Fifth Discipline that there is a need to understand before one can predict and influence organisational events. Learning to see underlying structures rather than events is of importance. Every individual has some competency or other. If human competencies are not used, they do not get developed or sharpened.

Natural resources limited, human ingenuity unlimited—use it. There is no going backwards for human being; the arrow of time goes only in one direction. Ralph Waldo Emerson had rightly told, "People sees only what they are prepared to see".

An HRD professional adapts the philosophy of kaizen (perfectionism), *mu* (openness) and *shibui* (sensitivity). *Mu* is a Buddhistic practice of remaining open and totally existing in the present. The individual or the collective mind is kept hollow and therefore takes in completely what is happening around it. Summarily HRD can be Buddhistic in content transcendental in action; so that action becomes formative, thought becomes normative and feeling becomes integrative.

Human resource generally means total quantitative and qualitative human asset or peoples in a society. Development in this context suggests all the formal and informal processes by which individuals learn. HRD therefore is developing parents to their maximum potential and also simultaneously conserving their talent. Professionally HRD can be:

Preventive— in arresting obsolescence;

Curative— in proactively bridging insufficiencies in knowledge;

Adaptive— in adjusting to socio-technological, environmental changes;

Promotive— in accomplishing excellence in quality;

Transformative— in making total man with men attributes (newage man).

Many professionals comment curtly that HRD is esoteric, it is all jugglery of words, sophisticated gospels, it is dumping department, it is human resource destruction etc. It is unfortunate on their part not to appreciate another profession. HRD is continuous creativity, reviewing all the time proactive human environment. It is a developmental step, in the process of human evolution, so that homo-sapiens transcend themselves and there is life-quality-improvement in the interest of mankind. Human beings, as individuals and also as groups are of crucial importance because the fruits of their labour are nothing but what we call family, society, culture, development, civilisation etc. HRD is a harbinger of new psychology; looks at things not as entities but in relation.

Man stands on the threshold of a big change. In the crucible of fleeting existence, man is required to be moulded to his natural self in order to meet the imminent change, the future.

Fissures in Man

Management instead of words, should be actions care for human development. Human perfectibility is the future of man. Evolving a conscious human relationship into a creative unity and harmony will be the future of man.

"We are all murderers and prostitutes—no matter to what culture, society, class, nation one belongs, no matter how normal, moral or mature one takes oneself to be". Ronald D. Laing regarded himself along with the rest of mankind, as prostitutes and murderers but is it all, about is? Certainly not. All these arise out of the fissures in man which prohibits man to be whole and to be complete, to be perfect. These fissures in human personality have to be overcome. Development of man is the first condition for the formation of perfect society. Man is our index and our foundation too.

When wisdom and sagacity arise there are great hypocrites. When family relations are no longer harmonious we have filial children and devoted parents. When a nation is in confusion and disorder, patriots are recognised. Similarly HRD comes to surface as a saviour to the perplexed man; the basic responsibility of the growing human being is to become himself inspite of the effect of external circumstances.

HRD Makes the New Age Man

Modern industrial societies depend on mega bureaucracies and microspecialisation of functions in order to coordinate and control their activities. Reg Revans, physicist turned his scientific mind to management and according to him, "Individuals need to learn at a speed that a greater than the rate of change if they are to survive in the long term".

To be earth citizen is to go beyond the present frontiers of consciousness which fragments everything and also divides the outer from the inner. Management can be development of man (free individual) the first condition for the formation of a perfect society. Management must aim at the developing and integrated man, a spiritual man, a perfect man and an individual. Such an individual will be constituting the future society.

Individual is governed by two factors namely inner and exterior. The inner factor (variation) is positive and creative producing all the raw materials for progress. The exterior factor (natural selection) is essentially negative and destructive, which eliminates harmful and less fit variations. Both these life and death forces are necessary for indivisuation of persons and organisations. Both these deep and surface structures are always at work. These are transformations and translations occurring simultaneously.

The fruits of HRD as a developmental management are horizontal participation and vertical learning with innovation. This development moves confidently towards the wholeness, both the individual and the organisation will continually renew themselves, there by actualising their interdependent potential. All entities large and small, public and private will both individuals and interfused on an ongoing basis. The managers shall draw behavioural, intellectual, emotional nourishment from their developmental roots like ecology, biology and psychology.

15

Towards Excellence in Administration Through HRD Interventions

Today's Administration and Administrator

Empires fall, ministers pass but bureaux remains. The administrative apparatus (bureaucracy) and the administrator defines the governance and ensure its continuity. Something more than mere inefficiency, redtape and rules have gone wrong. Is it that our political system and institutions have never matched our economic structure or economic institution?

The productivity in government organisations is low and their services are not worth the taxes and revenues they collect. This is primarily because its administration has accumulated too much fat and reasons for low productivity are due to:

- Constraints inherent in govt.; they seldom have clear goals;
- Responsibility and accountability are also unclear;
- Rules dominate over working culture and value system;
- Monopolistic structure and lack of benchmark;

- Political interference;
- Inadequate management techniques;
- Lack of awareness among those who work.

A combination of all these have resulted in low productivity. In administration, the inputs as well as outputs include both tangible and intangible components which cannot be easily segregated and thus are not amenable to measurement.

Maladies of the administrative apparatus are many, only a few of them are illustrated:

- Unresponsiveness to justified demands of time and situation;
- Tendency to regard itself as self-appointed;
- Self-imposed guardian and interpreter of public interest;
- Redtape or undue formalism;
- Punctilious exactitude in the observance of regulations;
- Departmentalism, empire-building and compartmentalisation;
- Splitting up the work into isolated self-dependent sections;
- Each section pursuing its own ends forgetting that they are only parts of the whole;
- Averse to change and pro-conservatism;
- Developing a negativity perpetually prone to prohibitions.

The administrator too has his own idiosyncrasies which when operate in conjunction with the apparatus can only be aweful! A few of these have been enlisted which are experiential (all 'he' can also be read and 'she'):

- He is abominable 'no man'. No changer, no pro-changer;
- He is nameless, faceless and soulless and likes these attributes;

- He is authoritarian, power crazy, monopoliser;
- He is aloof, remote formality, people environment and social dynamics;
- He is unresponsive and unresponsible too;
- He is a precedent worshipper and his sight is set to dead past, not to future;
- He is status hungry and strongly believes in hierarchy;
- He is a votary of red-tapism and file-fetish too;
- He is a conformist (sail with the wind). No self immolation, no martyrdom;
- He is self-perpetuating (officials make and work for each other);
- His favourite past-time is noting and drafting; revising, redrafting, rewriting and getting retyped as much as he can;
- His game-plan; let somebody else be scapegoat why you?
- He always plays safe; no extra dynamism, no entrepreneurial thrust;
- He excels in anonymity;
- He preaches merit but practises opposites;
- He lives in a sheltered world of its own (insulated and quarantined);
- He believes in preservation reservation and conservation (of self and system) but does not believe in delegation;
- His virtue is self-aggrandisement (inherent lust for power);
- His has faith in "If can be postponed not to act now". "Tomorrow will take care of today so wait till tomorrow", "Walk, never run, delay as much as you can";

- His trait is to pass the buck;
- He suffers from a syndrome "If you can say 'no' never say 'yes';
- His article of faith is rule-mindedness'; if a rule suits he can be deaf, dumb and blind.

In an interesting article Gerald E. Caiden writes how malperformance is increasingly being taken for granted and these vices, maladies and sicknesses of administration constituting what he calls 'bureaupathologies' have been enlisted under Table-C.

Based on the interaction between the administrative system and administrator, the latter can be of three types:

- *Egoist-arrogant variety:* Where the administrator is a beneficiary of the system. He is showered with out of turn benefits, like a house or a telephone or perks;
- *Sympathetic variety:* Often they are the denied or deprived of their legitimate claims. They are harassed through a witch-hunt campaign;
- *Pragmatic variety:* They are neither beneficiaries nor victims of the system.

They get their due from the system but nothing more nothing less. They are more efficient and less greedy.

Moreover, the way one has been brought up at home, the way one is educated, the experiences in the formative years of life also act as inputs into ones into one's administrative culture. Value - baggage of one's parents also contribute to shaping one's administrative culture. A product of IIT, REC will, more often than not, turn out to be of different cultural mode than others who acquire qualification through second grade institution or through donations. One's administrative culture would depend on the facts whether one has acquired one's position in bureaucratic hierarchy by sheer hardwork or by one's political clout only. In selecting goals, an individual is influenced by his own value system which may be either of the two:

1. *Operative value:* Value assumptions/criteria according to which actions or choices are actually made;

2. *Conceived value:* Values which are taught by culture, religion and ethics and at times have little practical influence on behaviour.

Interestingly, if we look closely into administrative system we find:

- Many individuals do not have even full days work and fewer individuals can very well perform all the tasks provided the scope of their work is not so narrowly defined;
- A growing tendency these days for more and more decisions to be taken at higher levels than in past;
- Too many levels are involved delaying speed and quality of disposal;
- There is no clear enunciation of duties and requirements of jobs to be performed at various levels, with the result that there is an all-pervasive tendency to pass any paper sideways and upwards;
- Nothing dominates as a method of disposal of government business. Major factors responsible for excessive noting is due to the prevailing sense of mistrust and the tendency to diffuse responsibility;
- It is as though each person has his finger pointed at the next person...and no one individual can be pinned down.

The govt. decision making is linked with several factors like:

- Bureaucratic-politician relationship
- Pressure-groups within and outside govt. organisation
- Effective communication system
- Standardisation of rules and procedures
- Impartiality of implementation systems
- Competence and credibility of subordinates
- Senior-subordinate relationship
- Personal relationship at all levels.

The traditional govt. is designed for governance. People are frustrated with slow, unresponsive public administrative systems that soak up large exchequer money in return for poor service. A citizen is often treated by an administrator as a subject and not as sovereign. Whenever a citizen comes in contact he is made to feel small by being made to wait or go around in circles in the name of rule, the concept of service or customer satisfaction is alien to the administrative culture.

Two more observations are relevant for any HRD specialist:

- ARC (Administrative Reforms Commission, Govt. of India, 1973) recommended that there should be elimination of noting except certain cases confined to more essential matters where a record of decision and reasons therefore is necessary to be in record.
- Prayag Mehta (1968) in his report had interesting observations:
  - 76 per cent of top IAS interviewed could not recall any effort to develop their own staff to grow;
  - 86 per cent of top managers interviewed revealed that govt. employees lacked competence for handling the increasingly complex jobs in govt.

Tomorrow's Expectations

The world today is in flux, turmoil; also there are new opportunities in knowledge, technology and globalisation. Also, there are threats and confusions over values, institutions.

We have taken governance and govt. for granted for too long and even we have seen more govt. and governance. Now people seek the other extreme i.e. 'no government'. It is because govt. is not performing. Govts. of today have been accused of inefficiency, redtape, high cost, low performance even in their basic functions like security, public order, maintenance of public utility etc. Expectations from govt. is better service without additional taxation! The task the govt. is expected to perform and the way it actually performs have been changing over time. They have been changing in the USA, Europe, Asia and India too. Administration keeps the fabric of society intact; it can also be viewed as a game of chess, in which there are no right or wrong moves, but only effective or ineffective moves. The desk officer is to go beyond the limits of the desk. His perception in certain nomenclature requires change:

From present mind-set	*To new mind-set*
Advisers	Consultants
Administration	Management
Calculators	Computers
Proposals	Systems
Proforma	Printout
Deadlines	Critical path
Short-term	Long-term
Hierarchies	Networking
National economy	World economy
Industrial society	Information society
Either or option	Multiple option
Centralisation	Decentralisation

Tomorrow is already expedited in today and there has to be a fierce global competition based on sophisticated information dissemination technology. Govt. institutions, therefore, have to be flexible, innovative and adaptable in terms of work-culture to be reflected in decision making style.

Shift from 'position power' to 'relationship power'. Power and wealth will now rest on knowledge and information. The only empire that will survive in the 21st century will be the empire that you build in your mind. The new global leaders will be people who can transmit knowledge and power. Change and competition and unavoidable. It has started invading and winning through TQM (Total Quality Management), RE (Re-engineering), JIT (Just in Time) etc.

Future govt. is going to be 'entrepreneurial govt', which is not expenditure oriented but mission oriented, people oriented, result oriented and productivity oriented. The delivery service will then be effective in terms of cost of service, quality of service, quantity of service with an in-built style of situational decision-making. Entrepreneurial govt. always act as a catalyst 'steer more than they row'. Less rule, procedure and paper oriented. Instead of transforming govt. the revolutionary step is to 'replace' it. Based on the 1992 American concept of privatising govt. services, we in India have NGOs (Non-Govt. Organisations). They are not sovereign nor public authority.

Information dissemination, distance annihilation makes the decision making decentralised so that on the spot decision can be taken.

What is wanted is a government and a governmental system which is *small, strong, efficient, better and less governance.*

What HRD Can Do

Development is a lifetime process and it is natural that the administrators need to be periodically retooled and revitalised. In the human context it can be defined as the process of acquisition of competencies.

Directed changes of administrative culture takes long 'social' rather than short 'human' or 'political' time. For development administration, the most important objective is HRD and through which change in attitude and values is accomplished. Only the actions HRD expert take 'here and now' can create tomorrow's real promise. It helps people to become great human beings.

HRD expert is different from an academician. An academician does teaching to youth but HRD expert is aware of techniques, styles of andragogy (adult learning). The real laboratory for growing an administrator is the real work within the institution itself and he is to grow in merit, competence and vision. HRD man is expected to be a guide and catalyser of the discussion rather than an authoritarian communicator. There are unlimited subtle and critical dimension viz. To impart structured training, to bring out latent strength, to transform the inhibited to a more confident one, to make a good listener. As a result lots of empathy and courage is gained and the administrator can enter to the world of the other to understand the framework of his thought. HRD forges a confident sense of self and a horizontal vision of organisational life. It also develops practical skills and competencies needed to public leadership, which must be grounded in the quest for self-identity, self analysis as well as the transcendental quest for human dignity.

In our country HRD function is to some extent pursued in corporate sector but its perception in govt. hardly goes beyond training. The concept of HRD is shown under Table-A. Although administration in India has generally been criticised for its inefficient functioning disproportionate delay in taking decisions, ineffective implementation of the decisions and a general lack of direction and purpose; but any strategy for controlling and developing administration are dependent to some extent on the acquiescence of the administrators involved and they resist it. Bureaucrats resist change and control because they enjoy autonomy, they feel they know the best and they are their own masters.

There is a general fallacy widely prevalent in the senior circles of bureaucracy that the top level administrators do not really need any kind of training and that there is very little for them to learn. Administrator's attitude impede the effective development administration.

Every individual has some competency or other. If human competencies are not used, they do not get developed or sharpened. Value system is a holistic reality is meaningful only with reference to a pattern or complex. Value merely perceived and/or conceived is valueless. It must be lived. HRD has a role to play. HRD man is to know while interacting with administrators how their attitude, value and moral hierarchy depend on three major factors: socio-economic, type and extent of education received, professional ties of the particular individual. Value system of administrators at various levels of hierarchy need not be similar and can differ. Value gaps or differences of values pertain to differences in conditions of life viz. age, sex, education culture, religion and environmental conditioning: and thus there are variations in value system in each organisation. In order to measure the value system Milton Rokeach has worked out a standard psychological test of 18 values based on 5 assumptions (shown under Table-B).

TABLE—A

Concept of HRD

Activity level	Focus	Economic Clarification	Evaluation	Risk level
Training	Present job held by person	Expense	On the job	Low
Education	Future job for which person is prepared	Investment (short)	On future job	Middle
Development	Future organisational activities	Investment (long)	Impossible	High

TABLE—B

Milton Rokeach's 5 Assumptions and 18 Values

Five Assumptions

1. The total number of significant values is finite, indeed quite small;
2. Values are universal;
3. People differ from each other only in emphasis on each value;
4. Values are arranged hierarchically within a value system; and the importance of a particular value is determined by its relationship with other values;
5. Once a new value is internalised by the members of a society, it develops some degree of functional autonomy.

Eighteen Values

1. A comfortable life (A prosperous life);
2. An existing life (A stimulating exciting life);
3. A sense of accomplishment (Lasting contribution);
4. A world at peace (Free from world and conflicts);
5. A world of beauty (Beauty of nature and the art);
6. Equality (Brotherhood, equal opportunity for all);
7. Family security (Taking care of the loved ones);
8. Freedom (Independence, free choice);
9. Happiness (Contendedness);
10. Inner harmony (Freedom from inner conflict);
11. Mature love;
12. National security (Protection of the country);
13. Pleasure (An enjoyable leisurely life);
14. Salvation (Eternal life);
15. Self-respect;

(Contd...)

16. Social recognition (Respect, administration);
17. True friendship;
18. Wisdom (A mature understanding of life).

TABLE-C

Common Bureaupathologies

Abuse of-	Indecision	Overspread
power	(decidophobia)	Overstaffed
authority	Indifference	Paperasserie
position	Indiscipline	Patronage
Alienation	Ineffectiveness	Pointless activity
Arbitrariness	Ineptitude	Redtape
Arrogance	Inertia	Reluctance to take
Bias	Inflexibility	responsibility
	Inhumanity	decisions
Bribery	Injustice	delegate
	Insensitivity	Rigidity
Carelessness	Irregularity	Rudeness
Complacency	Irrelevance	Sabotage
Conspiracy	Kleptocracy	Scam
Corruption	Lack of	Self-perpetuation
Deadwood	commitment	Self-seeking
Delay	creativity	Self-serving
Deterioration	credibility	Social astigmatism
Discoutesy	performance	*(unable to see problems)*
Discrimination	initiative	Spendthrift
Exploitation	imagination	Superficiality
Extravagance	vision	Tampering
Favoritism	Lawlessness	Tokenism
Fear of change	Laxity	Unclear objectives
or risk	Malignity	Unfairness

(Contd...)

Fraud	Mediocracy	Unnecessary work
High-handedness	Mindlessness	Unreasonableness
Ignorance	Nepotism	Vanity
Illegality	Non-productivity	Vested interest
Inaccessibility	Obscurity	Vindictiveness
Inaction	Obstruction	Waste
Inappropriateness	Oversight	Whim
incompetence	Overskill	Xenophobia
Inconvenience	Oversight	

Other HRD instruments are digging into the body-mind ensemble by using ISABS T-Group analysis, Transactional Analysis (TA). Action Leadership (AL) etc.

People show their competencies only when they given certain amount of freedom and opportunity. However, in govt. which is inflexible and rule-bound the competencies of individuals do not get developed. They only become exercisers of whatever have already been laid down. Slowly they become pegs in the invisible machinery and lose their humanness such mechanistic treatment. Britishers are not wrong in their firm belief in the principle of 'training by doing' and learning from mistakes. It is widely held that administrative skill has an essential empiricity and is amenable to acquisition more through practice than by mere imparting of training. Ralph Waldo Emerson had rightly told. "People see only what they are prepared to see".

Job oriented workshop is also an instrument. At the very outset the mission (objective) of the workshop is to be clear. Mission is to be translated to measurable objectives or indicators of achievement. Each participant is to identify the objective of his own job and contribution expected from him to achieve departmental goal. Each member is to present his job objective to the entire group of his colleagues. Modifications of weaknesses, if any can be made based on open-house discussion. HODs need not be present in workshops because more often than not he inhibits participation of his subordinates.

For transformation into mission driven systems what may be required are: anticipatory, planning and decentralisation, Piecemeal changes and a few microlevel successes do not weld automatically into a system. In the context of HRD, administration development needs of various levels of administration at grass-root level employees can be categorised of which:

1. an individual has;
2. a group has;
3. must be met immediately;
4. can be met in the future;
5. requires formal education and training activities;
6. require informal developmental activities;
7. require on the job instructions;
8. require off the job instructions;
9. the organisation can meet best within itself;
10. the organisation can meet through outside agencies only;
11. an individual can meet in a group session with others;
12. an individual can meet only by itself.

In most public services we have too many supervisors and too few workers. It is therefore, essential to specify all activities and present activities if any, to be analysed threadbare. Specification of activities may not ensure performance but non-specification does more harm.

There is Confidential Character Roll (CCR) but in addition to it a periodical performance review can be thought of. The periodicity to be defined by the appraiser or administrator depending on the nature of govt. organisation, span of control, feasibility etc. He should take a review of jobs performed. Periodic reviews can develop and sustain motivation and competencies. The potential of performance appraisal system as instrument of HRD has not been realised in govt. systems. Promotions are time-bound and not performance-linked. HRD interventions in this specific area helps in the following ways:

- Insight into one's own job;
- The amount of support required or not required;
- To understand one's strengths and weaknesses;
- Blue-print to overcome weaknesses and encash opportunities and strengths;
- Learning environment and opportunity.

HRD need not be classroom training only. It may be conferring, group discussion, quarterly, presentation, sharing of experiences amongst colleagues or in the presence of external specialists, field visits etc. All these to be followed by preparing reports and action plans for better work. Training activities should not be confined to prescribed state national institutes only; it is all narrow. What is necessary can be listed as:

1. The person to be trained must feel the need for training before he attends. If he does not feel so, his boss should interact and help him 'to see' the need;
2. The timing of sending for training should not be imposed but at a time conductive to the person so that he is in a position to receive it;
3. After training, the person should be given opportunity and at least some facilities (if not all) to use his learning;
4. Learning at a late age is difficult but not impossible. If learning inputs are not practised immediately after training it may not settle down in mind and may become volatile;
5. Except for specific individual training as a cost saving collective training may also be encouraged.

Encouragement and facility to be given for self-development and further education like:

- Liberal grant of leave form study;
- Facilities of leave for attending seminars and conferences;
- Encouragement for doing original work/reportage;

- Reimbursing part of expenditure on professional books periodicals etc.

Conceptually, productivity in administration envisages a result-oriented situation and not an activity oriented situation. In administration, productivity embraces efficiency as well as effectiveness. In administration the term becomes an empty phrase that embraces almost any change for the better. While reflecting on productivity in administration, the interaction with the environment has to be kept in view. This may vary with:

(a) the efforts of administrator in meeting environmental requirements;

(b) changes in the environment that may be induced by administration;

(c) changes independently taking place in the environment.

There will be differing concern and importance for administration at different times. Administration which lacks productivity perspective will find difficulty in recognising and thus reacting to environmental changes.

Creativity in management may be either of the two:

- *Non-surgical:* Innovative, regenerative, creative thinking, turn around;
- *Surgical:* Redesigning of practices, procedures public policy, computerisation, discipline, modernisation, restructuring.

Main thrust for administrators should be: overallness, sense of horizontality, futuristic perception, productivity mindedness and systems approach.

Action Plan

(a) *Systemic change:* There is a need for systemic change in the hardware part. The hierarchy itself needs to be restructured. Although defining productivity is extremely difficult in public administration productivity in govt. can be improved by simply reducing the number of people doing the same amount of work. Certain action points can be:

- Overcoming rigidity;
- Sheeding conventional mask of bureaucracy;
- Adapt new management techniques;
- More human in dealings;
- Promote competions to improve productivity
- Job enlargement for those trapped in tedious positions;
- Offering new challenge;
- Giving public a higher quality of service at a lower price.

(b) *Commitment:* A commitment on priority (comparative importance) of each activity an administrator does and time frame for completion of each activity; identification of activities one is doing or not doing identification of competencies one has and also those, one feels the need be developed for better discharge of function are often found to be eye-openers.

(c) *Measures for Productivity:* A few illustrative suggestions for better productivity are:

To reduce:
— reliance only on specific officers and instead system disposal;
— number of levels of paper movement;
— proliferation of unnecessary paperwork in inter and intra sectional references;

To improve:
— speed-up decision making process and quantity of disposal;
— quality of disposal; wholesome decision-making;
— wider perspective instead of getting lost in petty details;
— enforcement of accountability;
— grounds for introduction of new methods, systems, aids.

(d) *Import Learning:* There are learning points from other countries too. In Canada only telephones are used for any kind of horizontal memos/consultations; no paperwork. Absence of status consciousness amongst officers of all levels have reduced written references. In Japan informal relations prevail over other kinds of formal fora. In Russia any attempt to pass the buck is discouraged and matters involving high policy are considered by a collegium of officers.

(e) *Sound Policying:* In policy making administrators must interact with other experts so that inputs be it sociological, anthropological or otherwise are available and decision makers can gauge the decision situation in its total perspective and get the 'inner soul' realities. There should be a constant search to find new ways to improve services to the people and boost up productivity.

(f) *Questioning:* Certain food for thought can be through questions like:

- Shouldn't there be organisational restructuring?
- Should there be life time employment at all?
- Should there be job security in changing scenario?
- Moving in the corridors with some files and papers, only sitting near the table and holidaying permanently was enough to claim one's salary but can it be afforded today?

A public servant is to ask himself:

- To strive for good name and reputation or for material advancement by any means?
- What I am going to do?
- What harm will be caused by my action and to whom?
- Is the action inevitable in the larger public interest?
- What steps are to be taken to minimise its bad effects?

- Would my action stand to close public scrutiny?
- Am I doing to others what I would not have them do to me?

New Public Management Approach (NPMA)

We in our country always search for a "precedence", "past draft", "earlier decision" etc. even in ordinary normal decision making process. Innovations and past practices are two opposite poles in approaching a task unfortunately 'past practices' approach has been the standard procedure in governmental work all over the world. Administrative action should be user-oriented. Expertise and authority should rest with those who are closer to the users/customers. Breaking from previous practice requires a special rationale. Ironically going by the previous practice is taken as logic and rationality itself! Whereas initiative and innovation are not.

There are two separate angles: the diagnostic angle of the problem that plagues our govt. offices is seen by taking administrator as the proxy of all govts. The perspective angle is to reinvent certain prescriptions like innovation and enterprise at microlevel; transformation into mission driven systems etc.

Drastic alternatives required to reinvent govt. and to make it work. NPMA may add a new leaf to traditional administrative system through:

- Empower citizens rather than simply serving them because the modern environment is becoming more and more complex;
- Competition between services should be allowed and institutionalised;
- Internal organisational readaptation measures should be followed by managerial approach through efficient use of financial and personnel resources;
- Less govt. these days stand for better govt. Therefore turning bureaucratic institutions into entrepreneurial institutions comes under NPMA and the 10 entrepreneurial characteristics are:

1. *Anticipatory govt.:* If doesn't wait for the crises to come to surface. They anticipate and act. It believes that prevention is better than cure the cheaper too;
2. *Catalytic govt.:* Defining problems and then assembling resources for others to use in addressing those problems;
3. *Community owned govt.:* Empowering the people and shedding off quite a bit of bureaucratic control of public services;
4. *Competitiveness:* Injects competition into service delivery. There may be variety of competitions as we are used to the monopoly service of government;
5. *Decentralised govt.:* With new information explosion and communication decision making is decentralised. Public organisation can exercise better authority;
6. *Enterprising govt.:* It doesn't collect taxes and spends but can earn. But can the present govt. staff be trained to be enterprising?
7. *Less govt.:* Less task. Idea is not to control but to have higher productivity at less cost. These ten characteristics together reinvent govts. to entrepreneurship rather than just add expenditure to give more services for better welfare;
8. *Market oriented govt.:* Makers, producers and consumers to pay full social costs of their activities;
9. *Mission-driven govt.:* Tries to get out of the spider-web of detailed rules, instructions or guidelines;
10. *Result oriented govt.:* Pay attention to outcomes and performances rather than on-lines rules about inputs.

Epilogue

An antiquated structure and a leisurely procedure and incompatible with fulfillment of the demands of future. The higher the standard of political productivity the greater will be the productivity of administration. Political stability is directly relevant to administrative efficiency and economic productivity. Productivity will be poor where politics is the game of moral degenerates and administration is largely inhibited by self-seeking, mediocre bureaucrats indulging in abuse of power.

16

Re-energising Organisational Power Through HRD

No business is meaningful without human factor. Any meditation on business creates ground for re-looking and re-doing various activities which have so far been taken for granted. Any enterprise has its early days, teething problems, pink of health, peak period, productivity times, withering days, sickness, old age, death. In its performing times when it does not perform there is a need to re-energise, to re-vitalise. In order to achieve over-all re-energising certain Re's are done, each of these is an instrument by itself viz. Re-engineering, Renewal, Revival, Restructuring, Retaining, Repositioning, Re-generation, Re-normalisation etc.

A Relook at the Business

Business is a process which converts a resource, distinct knowledge, into a contribution of economic value in the market place and its purpose is to create a customer.

What exists is getting old. What exists therefore is always ageing. Any human decision of action, however courageous or appropriate it may be, starts to get old the moment it has been made. What exists is likely to be misallocated. Unless management constantly works at directing efforts into 'revenue producing' activities, the costs will tend to allocate themselves by drifting into 'nothing producing' activities. Schumpeter't Theorem says that profit results from the innovator's advantage and therefore disappear as soon as the innovation has become routine.

Every business needs a core, an area where it leads. Every business must therefore Specialise(S), must obtain the most from such specialisation, that is it must Diversify(D). S & D defines the scope of business and determine the productivity. In isolation neither is seldom productive. Business also needs Integration(I). Integration may be forward or backward. Forward integration is proliferation from manufacturing to marketing and backward integration is concentration from marketing to manufacturing or from manufacturing to raw materials as the case may be. SDI are strategies of high impact with high risk. The strategies must be subjected to tests of economic result and risk.

Business is a phenomenon of society and it has the economic task of:

- Making the present business effective;
- Identifying and realising the potential;
- Making a different business for a different future;

The ideas of business sums up answers to questions:

What is our business?

What it should it be?

What will it have to be?

Right structure, although does not guarantee results but the wrong structure often aborts results and smothers even the best directed efforts. Therefore, no matter how well suited to the needs of today's business, organisation must be reviewed as the business changes. If the rate of change inside organisation is less than the rate of change outside, the end is in right. Business must try not to minimise risks. Minimising risk does not mean no risk. Any attempt to escape risk may ultimately land on the risk of doing nothing. Any action must not only minimise risk but also maximise opportunities. Opportunities may be of three kinds:

Additive: It does not change character of business; only exploits existing resources;

Complementary: It changes the structure of business. It is synergistic;

Breakthrough: Fundamental change in economic characteristic and capacity of business.

Modern business, however, has the competitive edge on the following (5s): *Seiri* (organisation), *Seiton* (neatness), *Seiso* (cleaning), *Seikestsu* (standardisation), *Shitshke* (discipline). In addition to the 5s, the latest approach is towards 6-sigma, i.e. to a production without defects, 3-sigma stands for 66,807 defects per million, 4-sigma for 6210, 5-sigma for 233.

Inside-out thinking, Outside-in thinking, Short term advantage and disadvantage, Long term advantage and disadvantage are essential in an era of low cost and high speed. Change has become a way of life for may companies. But is change the only way to keep pace with change? May not be. The opposite may be true. Change is a wave in the ocean of time. In short-term the waves cause agitation and confusion. In long-term, the underlying currents are much more significant. To cope with change one has to take a long-range point of view in order to clear the basic vision and stick to it. Changing the direction of a large company is like trying to turn an aircraft. A turn means kilometers and if it is a wrong turn, getting back on course takes even longer both in time and distance. In such a detour worthwhile in a business? A company must point itself in the right direction.

Futuristic HR

Concentration is the key to success. Gone are the times when men were treated as commodities or another factor or production. Now they are @ the heart of business. HR must be concentrated on major opportunities, which are indeed very few. Concentration on 'these few activities' gives significant business results. HR is becoming her (electronic HR). There will be no files, no cabinets, no forms, no papers. People are now coming and asking will you show us the way?

Many managers are elated about their immediate tasks only. Many managers are knowledgeable (having knowledge without utility) but for business success. Knowledge must first be meaningful to the customer in terms of satisfaction and value. Knowledge is a perishable commodity. It has to be reaffirmed, relearned and re-practised all the time. Every knowledge ultimately becomes obsolete. Need for something different is felt. Knowledge has to progress to remain knowledge. It is like an athletic record which is crossed over by jumping a little higher or running a little faster. Executives, however, are the monarchs and manipulators of the 'present' only; neither they give sufficient time nor thought to the 'future', This is a neglect for which they and their business may have to pay a price. The executive has to accept responsibility for making the future happen. Executive has to be a business builder.

Tomorrow always arrives unfailingly. It is new and different:

- Future cannot be known. Future shall be different from what it is now. Future will be different from what we except;
- The hard realities of the present must not be obscured by the lure of tomorrow's promises;
- The difficult and risky work for tomorrow must not be smothered by the urgencies of the present;
- Basing today's action and commitment on predictions of future events is futile;
- It is worthwhile to anticipate future effects of those events which have already happen irrevocably;
- Making the future happen is definitely risky but rational;
- Risk is much better than comfortable and routine assumption;
- Making future happen is not what should be done tomorrow but what should be done today to have a tomorrow.

Disagreements are important. Decision through acclamation is more dangerous than through questioning. Products and processors are only the vehicles through which an idea becomes effective. Idea has power. If the idea is not both 'uncertain' and 'risky' it is not a practical idea for the future because the future itself is both uncertain and risky. Future cannot be based on risk-free ideas that cannot fail. Redefine yourself: What are you? Supposing is good, but finding out is better" thus said Mark Twain. Some ambitious, intelligent people find themselves trapped in situations where their future looks bleak. What they generally do is to try harder. What is needed is find a horse to ride. And your own company is the first horse to ride. Where is your company going? Or more impolitely it is going any-where at all?

2nd to ride is an idea

3rd horse is the faith

4th to ride is yourself

Like life itself, business is a social activity. As much cooperation as competition. Most people are 'un-sane'. They are not completely sane and they are not completely insane. They are somewhere in between. Insane person tries to fit the world of reality to the opinion in his head. Sane person constantly analyses the world of reality and then alters the opinion in his head. Un-sane person finds facts to verify his opinion; often accepting the expert's advice without even bothering for the facts at all. It is easier to be insane than sane. However, to be successful in the positioning era:

- you must be brutally frank;
- you must try to eliminate all ego from the decision making process. Ego clouds the issue;
- you must begin advancement in a small way and with the individual people need to be developed in initiate change;
- forget not that learning is coping and coping is survival;
- business is no longer directed by individual intelligence but by intelligences interacting and ceaselessly influencing one another;

- great plasticity is required to deal with beings' complexity. Musty technological advancement swell man's ego and shrink his conscience?
- should man be a commodity which is kept motivated only through payment?
- knowing the other person's self is of crucial significance.

Rational management is administratively oriented whereas developmental management is humanistic in essence. Rational manager value organisational manager whereas developmental manager values the whole man. The real management is balancing and integrating through HRD which is simultaneously.

Preventive: in arresting obsolescence;

Curative: in proactively bridging insufficiencies in knowledge;

Adaptive: in adjusting to socio-technological, environmental changes;

Promotive: in accomplishing excellence in quality;

Transformative: in making total man with new attributes (new-age man).

The shift is on from the 'position power' to 'relation power'. Power and wealth have started resting on knowledge and information. The only now is the empire but in the mind. The new leader has started transmitting knowledge power. To re-energise their inherent competency of human beings are to be used, developed and sharpened through T-group, TA, AL instruments. People show their competencies only when they are given certain amount of freedom and opportunity.

Life time employment and job-security are becoming obsolete in view of de-jobbing. Through change in mind-set and also in the work system re-energising can be achieved and for this the requirements are:

- Systematic change
- Commitment on priorities
- Import learning

— Sound policing

— Constant search

— Questioning

Human behaviour is too often been shaped by guilt and negativity, it is time to lift this dark cloud through positive revolution. Human thinking plays a central role in human happiness and development both from moment to moment and also over the longer term. Re-energising is a revolution, a positive revolution as Edward de Bono calls it where:

- instead of attack there is construction;
- instead of criticism there is design;
- instead of water logic there is water logic;
- instead of centrally organised system there is self-organising system.

If uses power of perception, information and effectiveness. It has five principles:

- *Effectiveness:* The greatest dreams remain as dreams only if there is no effectiveness. Effectiveness is a skill that we can build up for ourselves we only need the will to do it. Effectiveness is more admirable than intelligence. Effectiveness is setting out to do something and doing it. It needs 3 things; control, confidence and discipline. Set yourself small steps and carry them out. Effectiveness is not simply a matter of energy and action. Thinking is also required;
- *Constructive:* It means action, building making things happen—but always in the positive sense. Energy and activity by themselves are not constructive when we put together constructive and contribution that we begin to operate the positive revolution. Everyone can be constructive even in tiny ways. Being constructive means having positive expectations not of what may happen to you but of what you can do. Not every action is equally effective. Energy can be wasted so we do need to think carefully about the design of our actions;

- *Respect:* It is treating each other person as a human being with the dignity of a human being. It is treating others as you would wish to be treated yourself. It may be low or high. It is a scale. Organisation remains as an organisation because of the concept of respect for basic human rights that is respect. The expression of degree of respect is also a very powerful weapon in the way people can affect the behaviour of other people. A person because of selfishness might have minimal respect and another who contributes may have high respect;
- *Self-improvement:* It is day to day, slow process. It is to be there all the time. Developing positive attitude is the first step towards positive revolution. Taking interest in more things. Opening up your mind to new things. Becoming more interesting in your conversations and discussions. Pausing to access what you are doing. Being more tolerant of other people than critical. Not taking offence so easily. Involvement and adventure keep the mind young and energetic;
- *Contribution:* It is to set an example that can spread to other people. Constructive contribution can be a hobby. It can be to the levels of self, local, country and world. Some have special talent to contribute others have special position to contribute. Contribution is much more than playing with rules. It gives a basis to the judgement.

The positive revolution is based on individual people, their attributes and their perceptions. The power of the positive revolution comes from positive and constructive attitudes together with an emphasis on effectiveness. The power is not just the power of a group of people but the personal power that arises from being positive and constructive.

Use of AI (Appreciative Inquiry) often helps in re-energising. It focuses on generating and applying knowledge that comes from inquiry into moments of excellence, periods of exceptional competence and performance. From these moments we identify our lifer giving forces of sustaining and building ourselves. It is capable of giving a major shift in the practice of OD and transformation. AI involves, in a central way the art and practice of asking questions that strengthen a system's capacity to apprehend, anticipate and heighten positive potential. The five disciplines as conceptualised by Peter Senge i.e. personal mastery, shift in mental models, shared vision, team learning and systems thinking are all ingrained in the AI.

Talent is not a cheap commodity. Identifying the talents from the surplus manpower and to find how such talent could be fitted to new opportunities re-energises. The remaining surplus is definitely redundant. If possible they should be taught new skills to make them employable. Of course, it is not so easy to teach an old dog new tricks.

Through QWL (Quality of Work Life) re-energising can be done. QWL is a process of work organisation which enables its members at all levels to actively participate in shaping the organisation's environment, methods and outcomes. It is measured on nine dimensions adequater and fair compensation, freedom from excessive supervision and control, autonomy at work place, appreciation of ability and talents, challenging work, variety of work, growth opportunities, workers involvement in decision making, congenial work environment and working condition.

Epilogue

While the traditional management can and should continue to play their part, it is developmental management that is now required to take lead not only in India but also anywhere wherever there is human existence. Learning in the linear way is normal but then by unlearning and creating one can go beyond the traditional mainframe. We must demonstrate that we are still capable of creative regeneration and that we can develop a new path into the future that stands before us in all mastery and majesty. Modern industrial societies depend on mega-bureaucracies and micro-specialisations. It is rightly said that individuals need to learn at a speed that is greater than the rate of change if they are to survive in the long term.

Management can be development of man, the first condition for the formation of a perfect society. Management must aim at developing an individual who is an integrated man, a spiritual man and a perfect man. This earth citizen will go beyond the present frontiers of consciousness and such individual will be constituting the future society.

An antiquated structure and a leisurely procedure are incompatible with the fulfilment of the demands of the future. Let us not forget what Einstein said, "A hundred times everyday, I remind myself that my inner and outer life depended on the labours of other men, living and dead, and that I must exert myself in order to give in the same measure as I have received and I am still receiving".

17

Growth Through Learning

The Irreducible Element

Individual is an irreducible element by itself. All solutions are not outside but inside us. Instead of searching for solution outside we must try to forge solutions inside. Undoing of the you which is an obstacle against your own growth, you will transform your life at home and at work. Pressing the undo button in the computer key board takes no time but on the macro scale of our lives it is not instantaneous. While undoing we learn to find a quiet eye at the centre of our varied roles. Clearing the mental dross is crucial.

Every problem has a solution in it. There are situations when one distrusts good intentions, selfless actions. Such individuals fail as human beings and become miserable. To know what to give up is more important to than to know what to do.

Jack Welch said, " we must face reality as it is, not as we wish it to be". Knowledge (human capital) as an asset will supercede all other assets material and financial.

The Gyroscope of Business

Any business organisation need to have a business theory which has 3 parts:

- there are assumptions about the environment of organisation: the society and its structure, market, customer and technology;
- assumptions about the specific mission of the organisation;
- there are assumptions about the core competencies needed to accomplish the organisation's mission.

The first one defines what an organisation is paid for. The second defines how it envisions itself making a difference in the economy and in the society at large. The third where an organisation must excel in order to maintain leadership.

The assumptions about environment, mission and core competencies must fit reality. The assumptions in all these three areas must fit each other. The theory of the business must be known and understood throughout the organisation (inculcating a culture). The theory of the business must be tested regularly (as it is not permanent graven on tablets of stone).

Being human artifacts all theories of business do not last long they become obsolete and invalid. The first reaction of obsolescence is a defensive one, next reaction is to patch up. Both do not work. Rapid growth, unexpected failure or success are also other symptoms. When such symptoms are there it is time to rethink and identify the cause out of the three assumptions or a combination of two or more.

It is not cleverness but for the conscientiousness we all are paid for. It must not be forgotten that a degenerative and life-threatening disease will not be cured by procrastination. It requires a surgeon's time tested decisive action.

In 1977 Kenneth H. Oslen, erstwhile President of Digital equipment corporation announced that, "There is no reason for any individual to have a computer in his home". If Oslen had tried to understand the scenario he would have probably replaced Bill Gates. Uncertainty is the inability to predict an organisation's environment accurately due to lack of information or inability to distinguish between relevant and irrelevant data.

There is no proven track record nor any handy formula for organisation to succeed. The 3 drivers are:

Leadership:	Transforming
	Personal maturity
	Generate and sustain trust
	Clear articulates vision and thinking
	Clear, inspiring and effective two way communicator
	Strong sense of purpose
Strategy:	Make the organisation different by giving it unique position
	Meet customer's cross-cutting needs
	Power of analysis
	Unlearn the past
	Alternative strategies
Organisation:	Experimenting
	Sensitive to environment in order to learn and adapt
	Tolerant of unconventional thinking
	Living, learning and future focused
	Proactive and opportunistic

Any business is like a gyroscope, the dynamic wheel is always on the move against all odds, rock and roll of the ship. The nomenclature of words are also on move from left to right like the short listed few:

People	knowledge workers
Technology	information technology
Innovation	renovation
Business strategy	business planning
Era of uncertainty	era of creativity
Enterprise	technoprise
Capability	mindset
Competition	co-operation

Real corporation	virtual corporation
Control	deploy
CEO	CTO (Chief Transformation Officer)
Managing	Leading

Transformational Growth

Future belongs to the unreasonable ones, those who look forward not backward, who are certain about uncertainty and who have the ability and confidence to think completely different. When the going is good, move on. Look elsewhere, do something new, well before the situation worsens. To stay where you are is the surest path to oblivion.

Managers must simply learn to love changes as much as they have hated it in the past. Putting uncertainty through the lens, seeing it microscopically and telescopically is the want of the day. The organisation appears to us as it does because of the particular instruments we use in seeing it. Change the instrument and you change your perspective.

Learning and development is the keys to success. Three aspects necessary for an individual to be able to achieve any goal:

- willingness to act;
- focus;
- ability;

Abilities and capabilities can be enhanced at three levels:

- knowledge level through reading;
- skill level through training;
- attitude level through introspection.

Learn the art of learning and you are on the way to achievement. However it must not be forgotten that whatever made us successful in the past won't in the future. Learning organisation is seen as a response to an increasingly unpredictable and dynamic business environment. A learning organisation is not about mere training. A learning organisation involves the development of higher levels of knowledge and skill through four levels:

1. Learning facts. Applies to known situations where changes are minor;
2. Learning new job skills. Applies to new situations;
3. Learning to adapt. Applies to more dynamic situations;
4. Learning to learn is about innovation and creativity.

Learning organisations are those which make honest approach to challenge all that exists in the form of structures, systems, methods, rules etc. and empower people to plan the future of the organisation.

The importance of a clearly stated mission is often not understood. Many organisations lose good people not because of compensation but because people are unclear about the plans and future of the corporation.

Organisations consist of four kinds of people: *winners* (who stay motivated all through), *rebels* (who wish to change things but do not have the power to do), *non-contributors* (those who wish to contribute but cannot due to lack of skill and knowledge) *indifferent* (critical and apathetic never care what all are happening in the organisation). The later three are ambivalent who need to be communicated.

Realisation has now drawn that centralisation of power does not work. It only breeds alienation. The answer lies in giving power to the people through learning organisations.

In order to understand growth we must know why the companies, die. Companies die because managers focus on the economic activity of producing goods and services and they forget that their organisation's true nature is that of a community of humans. Profit is not a predictor or determinant of health but a symptom. What is important is organisation's ability to grasp environmental changes and adapt to them. Species behaviour rather than environmental changes alone was the major driving force behind evolution.

Institutional learning requires bringing people together so that learning can be disseminated through them. That in turn, requires an organisation that is tolerant giving employees a certain kind of freedom to experiment without fear of reprisal.

Art of Learning

Heraclitus said, "You could never step into the same river twice... it was forever changing, as was life...". Organisation is often misunderstood as a confinement where freedom does not exist. It is not true. To free ourselves from the cover of our own thoughts is real freedom. We can be reborn fresh every moment of our existence if we want. Choice lies with us only. Take everything in as if seeing for the first time.

Many of us still believe that future is a linear extrapolation of the present. Linearity simply does not exist. One small event may change the straight path in an unpredictable even devastating way.

World was never certain, will never be certain, only... is certain. Learning is the art of drawing sufficient conclusions from insufficient premises.

"Large organisations have to learn and innovate or it won't survive...it also requires something that is most difficult for existing companies to do: abandon rather than defend yesterday" thus said Peter Drucker. People think that businesses are made of 5 Ms but what is invisible is the idea, ideas expressed in words by human beings. Businesses are as successful as ideas. If ideas are outdated the business behaves accordingly.

In order to successfully evolve a learning organisation one of the critical issue is focusing on HR architecture. An intelligent organisation is a learning organisation, skilled at creating, acquiring and sharing knowledge.

Lateral thinking is a powerful instrument. While the normal vertical thinking opens new pathways along with chances of a maximum solution to a problem by challenging and provoking set norms and patterns. Lateral thinking skill does not impair the vertical thinking skill as it is based on concept breaking through provocation for allowing newer ideas through new patterns of thought. It allows innovative thinking and creativity through 'forward thinking' under which it will not be necessary to be logical or right but to be effective, even at a later stage. It is high time that concept divisions be set up which are as important as capital.

Learning the art of networking is also becoming critical to managerial success. It matters most in organisation that are:

- strongly decentralised;
- based on heavy interdependence between people of different knowledge and skills;
- based on common and demanding standards of performance;
- willing to allow leadership to be exercised by informal leaders;
- ready to accept challenges to traditional boundaries.

In networking one has to draw one's own personal network. The person with whom you do not speak directly is not in your network. Network relationship may be virtual, the members do not meet physically but network purpose is fulfilled through electronic or other kinds of communication. Networks are a recipe for personal and organisational success. Nurture yours and it will repay you many times over.

Appreciative Inquiry (AI) is another instrument which focuses on generating and applying knowledge that comes from inquiry into moments of excellence, periods of exceptional competence and performance. From those moments we derive life giving forces of sustaining and building ourselves. AI enables organisations to builds their own generative theory for enabling transformational shifts by learning from their most positively exceptional moments. Thus the organisations evolve themselves as learning organisation building on the appreciative learning culture. Such a culture develops specific competencies: affirmative, expansive, generative and collaborative AI also integrates the 5 disciplines conceptualise by Peter Senge viz personal mastery, shift in mental models, shared vision, team learning and systems thinking.

Self transformation in terms of higher values is essential to bringing organisational transformation. Man is the fundamental unit of the family, society and organisation. Unless his actions and behaviour change all efforts to transform organisation will bear no fruit. Changing our inner world of ideas changes the outer world of events. When individuals work for self change with tenacious and determined will, then only does organisation change.

Throughout history revolutions, whether technological or human, have emerged for the ultimate quest for personal freedom. Individuals who control their own lives feel better and produce better results. Today in the work place TQM and BPR promises individuals the control of these new systems architecture, using PCs promises them the support of information for that.

Knowledge is the Edge

Knowledge is the edge that differentiates the learning organisation from others. It is the indicator of growth. The process of creativity, innovation and knowledge management can be sharpened and put on a fast track, if the organisation is able to move its postures towards a learning organisation. Let us therefore be a party to the growth in a learning organisation where:

- Thinking is encouraged;
- Mistakes are seen as opportunities to learn;
- Tasks are assigned with development in mind;
- There are ongoing opportunities to expand knowledge and skill;
- New emerging technologies are sought after;
- Moves from prisons to possibilities.

Let us have hard look at the prisons we have created and a fresh look at the possibilities that stand before us. Growing with a learning organisation will make us more soulful, more vibrant, and we get a more meaningful lease of life while being a member of the organisation.

18

Of Birds and Men

We don't have time to observe of nature like the sounds of a flowing river or the falling leaves in autumn, colours of the flowers, ways of the birds and the bees. But we have time to book air-conditioned resorts for freaking out in the name of yoga and meditation, purchase highly advertised remix-salvation packages etc. Aren't we going away from nature? What follows here is a rethinking.

Like men birds too are found throughout the world. Birds like men are largely diurnal creatures and share with us the familiar daytime world of colour and sound. Man's association with birds is a long and peculiarly intimate which is one-sided. Man has worshipped selected birds, used them as symbols of empire, courage and prowess in his art, also hunted them for flesh and plumage.

In general birds are:

- Effortless
- Endlessly flexible
- Excellent aerial masters

Most birds seem to enjoy each others company but the birds of prey e.g. eagle live in solitary splendor like men. Eagle is a master diver and a master hunter like men. Large birds demonstrate magnificent majesty in flight. They have an almost effortless mastery of the air. Both sexes display by soaring to great heights.

Man shares the air with birds. Man cannot fly like birds but emulate gliding and flapping from the birds and apply as per his requirement.

Birds exploit the air current gliding down from a faster to a slower current, then turn to rise against the wind almost similar to a cyclist using his momentum at the end of free wheeling downhill to take him up across the next slope. Flapping, however, demands strong breast muscles for downward and forward feat. Long distance use this.

Large birds dive with the feet first then wings half-closed making a tremendous splash and rises almost at once. They have tremendous control on their body but men always miss the centre of gravity of their bodies.

Birds have more sensory cells in its eyes. They have a keen vision. They have a keen vision. Their eyes can see large and small. They are able to register and react instantaneously to far objects and near ones. Ordinary men lack these but can develop the skill from the birds. Eagles don't have the eyes of an owl. Eagles don't fly in dark but owls do. So are the movements of men. Everyone is different from the other.

Some birds can be tamed. It is through appetite principally that they are tamed to fit them for use in the field. It is not so much applicable for man. Today for both of them patience, care gentleness and training are equally necessary. Whether it is an adult eagle or an adult human being making them fit to meet the expectation is definitely a complex process. An eagle is a creature of excellence, intelligence and skill. Why not observe an eagle:

- From a height of 5 km an eagle focuses on its prey.

  Taking a bird's wholesome eye view especially for our long range objectives.

- An eagle dives fast while attacking the prey.

  Working at the peak of ability makes us more capable.

- An eagle does not eat a dead prey.

  Living on up the date and fresh information makes us more contemporary.

- An eagle soars high.

  While being a part or team one can soar high on individual strengths.

- An eagle goes up and up with the hope that the day has many promises.

  Every daybreak has an intrinsic optimistic mode, man should discover it.

- Bird is an air cooled creature.

  Thinking himself as a lightweight, air-cooled engine man can de-stress.

Man cannot relieve himself out from the self-created and soul-degenerating cesspool of avarice, bias, corruption, erratic behaviour, frivolousness, guilt, injustice, meanness, prejudice, revengefulness, selfish, wickedness etc. After all man is an admiring enemy of the other not found amongst the birds.

Life is either a daring adventure on nothing. It is never late to begin anything. Why not take life afresh one day at a time. Let us not remain away from nature. After all nature is larger than life and from which life gets its sustenance.

MISSION OF PERSONNEL

(Code of Conduct)

Dos

1. Uphold the honour and dignity of the profession;
2. Recognise and accept the dignity of an individual as human being, irrespective of religion, language, caste or creed and strive for the development of his/her personality;
3. Take keen interest in the establishment of healthy personnel practices and development of the profession;
4. Strive unceasingly to acquire ever changing professional knowledge, skill and experience;

5. Endeavour to eliminate misconceptions and misunderstanding about the profession, if any;
6. Express opinion on professional maters only when it is founded on adequate knowledge and honest conviction;
7. Maintain high standard in integrity and behaviour as the keynote of professional conduct;
8. Perform duties with all fairness, impartiality, fidelity, dedication to the cause of the profession;
9. Be a responsible member of the management team committed to the achievement of the organisation goals;
10. Try to win confidence and gain respect of the employers and employees while providing formal and informal interventions for resolving industrial conflicts;
11. Maintain at all times an open mind with regard to the problems with a view to understanding and resolving conflicts;
12. Enhance the good name of the profession in dealing with other professional bodies, government departments, and employers' and employees' organisation;
13. Co-operate in maximising the effectiveness of the profession by exchanging freely information and experience with other members and by contributing to the development of profession to the best of ability;
14. Give credit for professional work to those whom it is genuinely due;
15. Follow professional principles and practices tactfully and courageously keeping in mind the principles of equity in the fair distribution of work and rewards;
16. Promote such concepts, methods, skills, techniques in the field which contribute to productivity growth, profitability and employee satisfaction.

Don'ts

1. Not to disclose any information of confidential nature that may be acquired in the course of professional work without obtaining the consent of those concerned and shall not use any confidential information for personal gains;
2. Not accept or offer any improper gratification in any form or manner whatsoever in connection with or in the course of professional work;
3. Not take or acquiesce in any such action which may bring the profession into disrepute;
4. Not to damage, directly or indirectly the professional reputation or practice of other fellow practitioners;
5. Not to criticise the work of other fellow practitioners of the discipline;
6. Not to allow anything other than professional interest to interfere with the official work;
7. Not to interfere with the right of association of the employees;
8. Not associate with another co-professional who doesn't conform to the ethical standards.

19

Reverting Back to Kautilya and Sun Tzu

Even today, the works of Kautilya and Sun Tzu provide much food for thought in the day-to-day life of every person. Although it is not necessary that one should agree with each and every thought of theirs, yet so long as politics remain the most powerful determinant of collective life, their thought will continue to be of value.

Kautilya

Circa 400 BC. Born at Chanaka near the confluence of the rivers Kabul and Sind, dearly known to his parents as Vishnugupt, he became famous as Chanakya. He was born to *'kutala' gotra,* hence, came to be known at Kautilya. He was dark, learned, orthodox Brahmin highly versed in politics. He served the Nanda King of Bihar (Magadha), but on being alienated, he instead served King Chandragupta during 321-296 BC to trounce the Nanda kingdom. He had been instrumental in developing a service which would sharpen both wisdom and the weapon to meet the challenge with a strong political outlook and diplomatic principles to fulfil the mission of political unification of India, Machiavelli is often compared with Kautilya.

His treatise, the *Arthashastra* is not considered a part of *Dharmashastra* (scriptures), nevertheless, it is the greatest Indian treatise on the art of government and administration, the duties of the king, ministers and officials so also the art of diplomacy. Kautilya, in his treatise, appears to be cynical towards the expected behaviour of government servants. This cynicism is the main difference between *Dharmashastra* and his *Arthashastra*. Only a selected area of his thought is enlisted below:

1. *Man and Animal:* A person having faith is long living, and a faithless living is as good as dead. *Dharma* is unostentatious work. Only by shedding bodily ego, the mind wherever it travels finds deep meditational peace. Sense of understanding and *dharma* make men superior to animals;

2. *Learning:* Learning is like a *Kamadhenu;* it fulfils all desires and yields fruits at all times, it gives protection like a mother; it is like a hidden treasure. Men can also learn from animals and birds, *e.g.*, from a lion to act according to one's will, mind, and strategy; from a duck to keep all the senses under control; from a cock man can imbibe four qualities; to rise early, not to turn his back in the battle field, to share everything with fellow beings, to get one's need by attacking first etc.;

3. *King, Kingdom and the Statecraft:* In the happiness of his subjects lies his happiness; in their welfare his welfare; whatever pleases him (personally) he shall not consider as good but whatever makes his subjects happy he shall consider good. King should favour those who are contended with additional wealth and honour and to those who are discontended he should propitiate with gifts and conciliation, in order to make them contended. Not violating righteousness and economy, the king shall enjoy his desires. The king shall not only maintain his servants, but also increase their subsistence, and wages in consideration of their learning and work. For a king the only religious vow is his 'readiness to action'. Best talents should be groomed for administration either as advisors or as administrators. A wise king can make even the poor and the miserable elements of his

sovereignty happy and prosperous; but a wicked king will surely destroy the most prosperous and the loyal elements of his kingdom. A country which is thickly populated is a kingdom in all its senses. A king desirous of success or victory must be possessed of good character and of best fitted elements of sovereignty and thus he can be the fountain of policy. The road to success lies not through unlimited application of force involved in absolute or total warfare, without calculation of cost. It would be a negation of strategy and statesmanship;

Three stages of a State are: deterioration, stagnation and progress. The successful attainment of objectives by any State is dependent on two factors: peace and industry. Efforts to achieve the results of works undertaken (*vyayam*) are industry, and absence of disturbance to the enjoyment of results from work is peace.

Since human causes are controllable, efforts can be concentrated on them and by means of a wise and proper policy, human efforts can be successful;

4. *Conduct of Officials:* Just as it is impossible to not to taste the honey or the poison at the tip of the tongue, so it is also impossible for a government servant not to eat up, at least, a bit of the king's revenue. Just a fish moving under-water cannot possibly be found out either as drinking or not drinking water, so government servants employed in government work cannot be found out (while) taking money (for themselves). There are about 40 ways of embezzlement, it may also be much more;

5. *Espionage:* When the king has set spies on the high officials, he should set spies on the citizens and the common people also. Spies shouldn't know each other. Secret agents, opposing one another, should carry on a disputation at assemblies, communal gatherings, holy places and other congregations of people. One of them should say, "This king is said to be endowed with all virtues yet no virtue is to be seen in him as he oppresses citizens etc.", whereas the other should contradict him and some others should recommend either of the views.

Rasda (poison givers) can be those serving as cooks, waiters, bath-attendants, shampooers, bed-preparers, barbers, velvets, waterservers, *Tikhna* (a fire-brand, fearless and desperate with propensity for violence, taking pleasures in killings), *Bhikhuki* or a mendicant women or poor widow having access to the residence of officials often mixing with unsuspecting ladies, desperadoes serving as bearers of umbrella, watervessels, carriage, shoes, etc., should ascertain the outdoor activities of the officials. Snakecharmer, vintner, a procurer or pimp, a jester or joker, a musician in the company of prostitutes, astrologer, scholar, physician, blind, actors, dangers, a singer or a bard, magician, humpbacks, eunuchs, cook, masseur, women skilled in arts, dumb, dwarf, and petty merchant should be employed as spies among the enemies. A recluse or wandering mendicant or pseudo-ascetic with disciples on the outskirts of the cites and influencing the gullible with his gimmicks is also helpful for espionage work; they should be quick in their work to find news of the activity of the enemy. Espionage in the foreign country centres around political emissaries (*doot*) and the institutions of spies. The agents in foreign lands are to concentrate on those dissatisfied with their king of their homeland, or humiliated or exiled or wrongly imprisoned or fined, etc.;

6. *War and Peace:* Categories of policy may be of two kinds—peace and war. From these six distinct and mutually exclusive modes emerge, *i.e.* peace (agreement with pledges), war (offensive operation), marching (making preparations for war), indifference (neutrality), alliance (seeking protection from others) and peace with double policy (making peace with one and waging war against another). If the advantage from peace and war are weighed to be equal, peace is to be preferred, as disadvantages, such as loss of power and wealth, sojourning, and sin are ever attending upon war. It is power that brings about peace between any two kings (states), no piece of iron that is not red-hot will combine

with another piece or iron. By making use of conciliation and other forms of stratagems an agreement of peace is made; it may be peace for no specific end (other than self-preservation), peace with binding terms. Through the agency of traitors and spies, the agreement is broken by a treacherous king amounting to the breaking of peace. Reconciliation is made at a lower hierarchical level termed as restoration of peace. War is a continuance of state policy by other means (*upaya*). War must serve the ends of policy and must necessarily be conducted with a view to gaining post-war benefits. Dislocation and paralysis of enemy, tactfully, is preferred to destruction. A traditional friend close to the territory may be deemed to be a natural friend (natural can be interpreted as sworn and impeccable) while he whose friendship is counted for self-maintenance is an acquired friendship.

Sun Tzu

Circa 510 BC to circa 210 BC. Sun Tzu was a great thinker in China. He wrote his treatise Ping Fa (Principles of War or Military Strategy) in China when Buddhism, Zoroastrianism, and Torah were taking firm roots elsewhere. The central premise of his treatise is: Winning or losing depends on artful strategy, not military brown:

1. Cretins (stupid persons) around must be watched. Victory comes from cold-blooded tactics, not vulgar warrings. If you want to win first think it out;

2. Psyche your opponent out; make him blink and finish him off as he does so. Victory comes first, from knowing your own weakness, and if you cannot overcome them by baiting your enemy with them, to force him into making strategic errors from which you can gain. The tortoise wins not because of learning how to run faster than the hare, nor because it persists, as Aesop would have us to believe, while the lazy hare sleeps. The skills of the tortoise lies in fooling the hare, persuading the hare to believe that he (tortoise) is not a serious competitor at all, and thereby coax the hare into the fatal error of understanding his rival. That is what the strategy is all about;

3. Raising and marching a 100 thousand men great distances entails heavy losses of the people and drains out resources of the state. The daily expenditure will be of a thousand silver ounces and there will be commotion. Many will drop down dead. Hostile armies may face each other for years, striving for victory that will be decide in a single day. This being so, to remain in ignorance of the enemy's condition simply because one grudges an outlay of a hundred silver ounces in honour and emoluments to the spies, is the height of inhumanity. One who acts thus is no leader of men, nor can he help his sovereign nor attain victory;

4. Artful conflict manager rides chaos, to victory. To create chaos and then spur it on to his own strategic advantage contrary to most politicians who are unthinking creatures of habit who repeat old tactics in moments of crisis;

5. Five varieties of spying and five different spies are: local spy (belonging to enemy country but won over by kind treatment and enrolled as spy), internal spy (using enemy officers civil and military personnel as source of information), converted spy (using the enemy's spy by converting them into his own service through bribing, inducing them to carry back false information and spy on their own citizen/countrymen), condemned spy (spies captured by the enemy deliberately giving false reports) and ordinary spy (regular army spy);

6. War is a great affair of the state, the realm of life and death, the road to safety or ruin, a thing to be studied with extreme diligence. There are five threads to the warp of its texture—the ethnic (making people one with the ruler), heaven (divining the right moment to act), earth (knowledge of the terrain, ability to assess distances and time to cover them), leadership and material (morale of officers, drill, discipline of men and supplies given to them).

20

Seven Laws of Deepak Chopra and Seven Habits of Stephen Covey

Seven spiritual laws have been interestingly framed by Deepak Chopra for adults and also for seven more for parents.

For Adults Who Think

Law of Pure Potentiality: Realising our true self is pure potentiality and aligns with the power that manifests everything in the universe. To do that practise to be silent twice a day. To just be, commune with nature, practise non-judgement.

Law of Giving: Willingness to give that which we seek and doing that which keep the abundance of the universe circulating in our lives. To do that take a gift—a flower, a prayer whenever you go and whoever you encounter. Receive gratefully all that life has to offer.

Law of Karma: (Of cause and effect) when we choose actions that bring happiness and success to others, the fruit of our action karma is happiness and success.

Law of Least Effort: When we harness the forces of harmony, joy and love, we create success and good fortune with effortless ease. To do that practise acceptance of things as they are. Take full responsibility of ones situation and not blame anyone or anything for it; relinquish the need to convince or persuade others to accept one's point of view.

Law of Intention and Desire: Intention and desire in the field of pure potentiality has infinite organising power. To do, it is required to accept the present as it is and one should go on to manifest future through one's deepest, most cherished intentions and desires.

Law of Detachment: In detachment lies the wisdom of uncertainty. In wisdom of uncertainty lies freedom from our past, from the known, which is the prison of past conditioning. To step into unknown, to field all possibilities we surrender to creative mind. It means one should be "open to infinite choices", to experience all fun, magic, adventure of life.

Law of Dharma: (Purpose of Life) Everyone has a purpose of life—a unique gift or a special talent to give to others. When we combine this talent with service to others we experience ecstasy of our spirits.

For Parents and Their Children

The following seven laws are the parents' tool keeping in view to raise children with a true understanding of how natural universe works and the ways we can connect with it.

Everything is Possible: Child should think something which may be God has created and creates everything and that everything is possible in his life.

If Want to Get, Give It: Giving is the secret of abundance. Encourage child to give away something however small it may be to a family member, a friend or a teacher. Child should know that the parent appreciates the act of giving.

While Choosing, Future Changes: When you make a choice, you change the future. Ask children about choices they made at playground, shop etc. and how they felt about it good, bad, indifferent etc.

Don't Say No, Go With the Flow: If we have faith and patience good things will come to us. Life is not always a struggle to achieve things in specific time.

Wish Plants a Seed: Everytime you wish or want you plant a seed life is creative journey which can be fun and purposeful.

Enjoy the Journey: Do not put excessive pressure on yourself. Take a break purposefully and meditate to be with the Creator and His creation.

For a Reason We're Here: Materialism is not enough; it gives limited amount of satisfaction. Be helpful, be thoughtful and you get inner happiness.

Stephen Covery speaks of seven habits of highly effective people. He says, "So often the problem is in the system, not in the people, if you put good people in bad system, you get bad results". In families parents can shift focus from competition with each other to cooperation. In education teachers can set up grading system based on individual's performance in the context of agreed upon criteria and can encourage students to co-operate in productive ways to help each other learn and achieve. In business, executives can align their systems to create teams of highly productive people working together to compete against external standard of performance. The habits are:

- *Be Proactive:* To focus on a circle of influence to produce results rather than react, place, blame, point finger or make excuses. As people develop the habit of proactivity (being responsible for one's actions), they become more responsible. They stop complaining, begin to be innovative, look for the opportunity and contribute.
- *Begin With the End of Mind:* Identifying mission and values before setting goals, any effective personal and organisational development is principle-centred, value-driven and mission-oriented. Seek unity between means and ends.
- *Put First Things First:* To be priority oriented. Learn how to manage time and resources in ways that keep one focussed on key roles and goals, reducing wastage, increasing productive time through high-leverage activities.

- *Think Win-Win:* It teaches agreement and contract negotiation to see from the perspective of a win-win or no-deal, resulting in mutual satisfaction. This skill is applied to improve relationship in business, with colleagues, employees at all levels, suppliers and customers.
- *First Understand, The Be Understood:* Seek first to understand then to be understood. Empathy is the key to being able to understand and influence. When people feel understood, they are open to influence. Through this habit rivalry is reduced, team building is effective.
- *Senergize:* Once differences are valued working effectively together is successful. Greater organisational unity, reduced rivalry, high quality decision-making results in.
- *Sharpen the Saw:* Practise this so that people maintain balance and perspective. They learn to weigh today's outcome against tomorrow's potential.

All these try to provide a common language in solving problems like self-management, human interaction principles etc. and also encourages shared mission, values, strategy and goal in a more cohesive and functional way leading to powerful culture.

21

Think Before Changing A Job

Professionals at middle/Sr. levels in age group 35-45 are prone to change jobs either for:

- fast track career growth;
- better prospects;
- incompatible boss;
- office environment adverse;
- place of work/living;
- personal fortune making;
- improve professional exposure/skill;
- dissatisfaction with present structure;
- general nature of persons to enhance his status;
- discontentment with existing environment.

Process

- Many companies advertise. They sell a dream what it wants to be (rather than whom they want).
- Aspirants apply/respond through a well documented CV (curricula vitae) i.e. a careerography.

- Perusal interview. Lots of show off on both sides.
- Contract signed. Delivered.

Introspection and External Analysis

Aspirant is to analyse quietly certain critical factors.

1. Does it change location? If yes, will company take care of housing, transport, school admission.
2. Does the school syllabi compatible? If yes, OK, if no, can the children cope with?
3. A new job means to the family (even if they don't say) a bigger house, better school, a better car, higher standard of living, better society.
4. How is the social milieu at new location? Is it better than the existing or not? Or as good?
5. Does the change mean separation from family or shutting in between? In that case are you fit to live alone?
6. Can your family live independently? Have they lived in the past?
7. Whether arrangements made for family? Are your answers to all these questions satisfactory to your family?
8. Is your new take home salary at least 1.5 times?
9. Is there substantial and persistent/perceivable difference in your new job profile?
10. Is the responsibility—authority matrix, coupled with freedom of operation better than existing?
11. Is the new organisation comparable/better than the existing in respect of status, image in market, reputation, finance?
12. Can your change give you a meaningful opportunity to prove yourself?
13. How much the new company needs you?

14. Can the co-stretch to meet your expectations?
15. Have they not been able to find someone within the organisation?
16. How are you placed among others of comparable age and qualification?
17. Check the new chair, are there invisible thorns or a false cushion?

During the entire process before change.

Do not decry the existing old employer and after change.

Do not live in the past and think of future only.

22

Random Thoughts of a Manager Writer 1989-99

A manager is busy in managing; where is the time to write? All managers can't write. Only a few managers occasionally write to describe their experience, their wisdom, their feelings. This type can be named as managed-writer. His writings arise out of managing not the other way round.

This manager-writer whose thoughts are here had his grounding in physics who could very well have been a nuclear scientist culminating into a nuclear blast but after his induction and orientation in a large PSU he grew to be a manager instead, without any remorse whatsoever. While reflecting on his job, his peers, his environment etc. he had these writings which the present author feels will be interesting for all practising managers. It evokes twinges of recognition in all of us. It opens valuable insights for more joyous and satisfying life both organisational and personal.

15.6.89

Let there be a disclosure of my experience without any aspersion and prejudice. Joined a behemoth PSU. Colleagues are just above mediocres, not the top brass of university pass outs.

31.12.89

Peers and onlookers see new entrant as an apprentice, a future manager in the making, may be a contender.

1.1.90

They taught in training, without quoting Einstein, "Try not to be a man of success, but rather try to be a man of value". The general ethical paradigm took an industrial grafting. Training is a preparation for the show—the long show of 30 years ahead. There is no resistance, no rebellion, only a slow death, some where deep within.

15.6.90

Spent one year in organisation spent. Values like responsibility, integrity, commitment, honesty, morality still exist, as it appears. Any industrial society losing its moral bearing is surely heading for disaster because all failures are moral failures only, never structural or systematic failures.

16.8.90

To serve is to struggle.

17.10.90

Every effective executive is an autocrat.

30.11.90

Living and managing are intriguing. Many cannot integrate. They live a split-life.

3.12.90

Introvert managers are also listened by as many workers as the extrovert public-entertainer manager. Their styles of control are different. They are good observers and meticulous executors.

4.1.91

It is not at all wise to look confused or uncertain. An aura of expertise often helps.

16.4.91

Interestingly the future of business is unclear because of myriad external factors. Managers are paid lavishly for their highly finite and structured activities.

20.6.91

Even after decades of exercising management techniques command and control prevail. To control the 'untrustworthy' elements by dominance has left its scars of failure. That is a reason running the rat-race has become the ultimate objective of all managers and they give much less than what they are capable. Well intentioned efforts, if it is not a routine, repetition, is viewed critically by everybody at home and also at work.

1.10.91

When anything is executed firmly—the autocratic behaviour causes anger, the success breeds rivalry and jealousy. Others are involved but the rule is dictated by the manager, the ultimate success is claimed to be his. Accolades too are endowed upon him to reinforce such success!

11.12.91

Like a petty criminal once there is success in the act, however heinous it may be, the manager becomes addictive, highly active and excited to make things happen again and again in his favour.

28.1.92

To be more human and less lonely one has to be connected with others around instead of self-centred beast of burden. When the manager changes his own behviour everybody else around him achieve their full potential.

11.3.92

Nobody has the patience or the time to listen. Mental preoccupation has gone so high there is no end to it.

28.6.92

When the manager feels powerless, he lords over the supporting staff through anger and express his dark side. When the after-burst subsides every manager tries to rationalise such actions which indicates his guilt only.

12.8.92

In industrial societies additions are many: drinks, sex, gossip, backbiting. These are not uncommon elsewhere. These provide a convenient escape from 'real life'. Emotional growth is throttled. Nobody has the guts to face life as such. That is the reason everybody suffers during mid-life crisis till lost into oblivion on retirement.

29.10.92

Interestingly those who drink or do adultery without being talked around feel as if they are the most powerful, socially acceptable and rightfully controlling everything around them!

11.11.92

Emotional dissonance arising out of work life does disrupt the manager's evolution as a human being.

10.12.92

A manager can be soulful or soulless. Soulful when he himself is involved with the people and soulless when he watches the people racing like rats, for promotions, incentives, rewards etc. Soulless manager is inhuman—while seeing the fittest few surviving he has to see many unfits perishing. Such organisations cannot be called a living organisation. Development is absent.

3.1.93

Unless managers accept the information as a friend and cease to consider as an enemy there can't be a vision of the future. The key resource in 21st century will be information and knowledge, not the capital nor even the people.

31.3.93

Allowing the subordinates to perform at a higher level is of crucial importance.

4.4.93

Everybody wants action and result. All are busy, compelled to do even if it is needed or not, right or not. How often we "lift the lid" so that the people can reach their natural heights?

13.6.93

Whenever there is effort to rule by force by X, against the self-interest of Y there is sabotage. Managing becomes a farce.

30.9.93

The word 'unmanageable' does not mean 'failure' or 'unsuccessful'. It is only a bluntness without pinpointing the space or the time. It is a fleeting situation, none is responsible!

1.12.93

Controlled management behaviour when reflected elsewhere brings disorder. At home housewives bring order to such disorder; otherwise life itself would have been unmanageable and chaotic. Much of our life is beyond our control. It must be accepted as a fact of life by all managers. Other people, market, competition, recession etc. are beyond the control of any manager.

31.1.94

Human beings, more so the managers, have only responsibility not power. Power is a belief—which causes a fear for the powerful. Empowerment is entrusting more responsibility, allowing to own more.

13.4.94

Those who have power (positional power) are despised and held responsible for various problems in all fronts. Interestingly those who see themselves 'not in power' preach that all power corrupts and those in power are corrupt.

5.6.94

Very few managers check the following:

— are they spending a lot of time grabbing power?

— are they enjoying and sharing while using the power wisely?

30.9.94

No manager is perfect unless he suffers a sense of guilt and shame. Guilt arises from doing wrong things against others and shame arises out of self unworthiness.

12.12.94

It is a pity that managers do not have meaningful contact with wide range of people. They are only confined to the office, neighbourhood and shall social spaces.

31.1.95

Like the natural world, it is not that easy to clean up organisational pollution. Stagnation, disowning, isolationism, adhocism, human-misfits etc. add to the pollution of organisation. When the organisation gets choked, its life-line is to be restored to prevent premature dysfunction. Anybody taking care of this aspect of full-scale organisational clean-up? None.

7.5.95

When an organisation shall understand the wake-up call of the wise and caring man?

1.9.95

Even powerful and efficient managers avoid confrontation. They feel uncomfortable even by the idea of being out of control.

15.12.95

It requires real courage to extend unconditional support than to warn. Very few managers are courageous. Most are obedient cowards who fill the higher echelons of management!

21.2.96

Manager must discover the fact of his imperfection and come to practical term with it.

31.3.96

Reports are not facts. These are avoidances, insidious long-term illusions, obfuscations and lies too. Honest reporting often goes against the interest of the reporter.

1.5.96

Games people play can be meaningful with honest transactions and transparency. What is required is more information and less drama.

23.7.96

Even in a team trust is absent. One considers the other as a threat. Nobody likes to respectfully work together to harness the data for collaborative problem solving. Any team member not obeying the contrieved rules of obfuscation is discreetly counter-attacked, disciplined. As a result team meetings are quickly done away with and 'one-to-one with boss' culture takes over.

17.8.96

Competition in organisations are often clandestine or subtle. Collaboration and competition are different. Collaborative means co-operative, it even means to co-operate with enemy through treason.

23.9.96

Competition has an edge but collaboration has no edge.

12.10.96

Hiding the struggle or hoarding the learning helps in no way.

7.11.96

High performance multicultural systems can be created by right managers not pseudo-managers.

16.12.96

Courage for a manager can be: self-examination, inter-and intra-personal risk-taking, life-long commitment to learning and personal growth.

8.2.97

Boss-centered cultures are not conducive to high performance. When boss-management becomes the only management, nothing remains except mismanagement. Everybody becomes a time-server only.

22.3.97

Competition is for grades, for promotions, sports, to capture market etc. There is differentiation between winners and losers. There is a desire to control outcome and avoid failures. Competitions are carefully planned like a war or a construction activity.

30.6.97

When a manager's promotion is delayed a part of his good self gets amputed. How many personnel managers understand this? More stagnations, no promotions for years, juniors superseding seniors go on amputing the goodness till the manager is an irreducible non-entity!

10.10.97

May be best person win in rat-race not the fraud, not the careerist not the manipulator. Let the method go beyond the pass-fail appraisal. A barometer of work culture can thus be prepared.

2.3.98

Yes there are cut throat competition, price-rise, recession but in order to sustain people in the organisation innovation, risk-taking, creativity and performances must be ensured so that people come to work everyday to express themselves (not to prove themselves!)

7.6.98

Modern managers are to know how to take on-the-spot decisions taking into account all multifarious factors and understand how self-organising systems work.

8.8.98

If mistakes are covered with excuses to protect one's career, innovation gets killed. If promotions are limited, managers jump like dogs to get the limited bones thrown at them. How can there be a team!

1.10.98

If the organisation is a family how the family secrets go to the competition market, to the wrong hands!

1.1.99

Managers are asked to do more with less resource. They are under pressure to drop the shackle which is no longer working.

2.3.99

Often managers feel to make things happen including their own promotions, tours etc. Once they start ruling themselves they become autocrats or self-controlling. managers. Autocrat comes from Greek meaning ruling by oneself.

12.5.99

To be in charge every time and all the time is torture. It is like sitting on a volcano. Ironically, when it goes out there is conflict, there is insubordination, there is complacency. That is power and the taste of power.

17.6.99

The hard-hitting boss says 'no matter how hard you think you tried, if it does not work it was not enough on your part". This is demonstration of power and authority but often the managers forget that a horse can be brought near the pond to drink water but the horse can't be made to drink then and there.

24.8.99

Conversations often turn to accusations in work-life. Failures are dissected threadbare but never the success.

11.10.99

There is information boost. One cannot understand what the new-age managers are saying. Pace of change today is 5 times what it was 50 years ago! The minimum know-how is doubling every 7 years to come. To feel competent in the present day explosion of information is difficult.

3.11.99

There is less and less of wisdom, and less and less of courage among managers now. Aren't they necessary any longer?

24.11.99

The creative human spirit must be conserved. Let it is not be unleashed only for commercial use.

31.12.99

Creation of personal mission statement by individual manager is the only way to preserve his identity as a human being.

23

Total Quality Focus

The Total Quality Concept

It is an approach which involves people and process, products and costs, planning and management, in fact, ensuing quality in each and every sphere of organisational activity. Its main objective being to achieve quality at the lowest cost and to achieve this clear-cut plan to improving the quality of operation, development of all resources, optimisation of cost factors and though last but most vital is to win users' satisfaction.

Since steel and machine tool industries have been identified as priority areas where quality improvements will result in significant benefits for the rest of the industries the needs of the users play a crucial role for the existence of a business enterprise like a steel plant. Quality, therefore is not the business of a quality control laboratory alone but everybody's concern.

Our Business as a Process and Challenges Ahead

The block diagram of steel industry as a business process is show below:

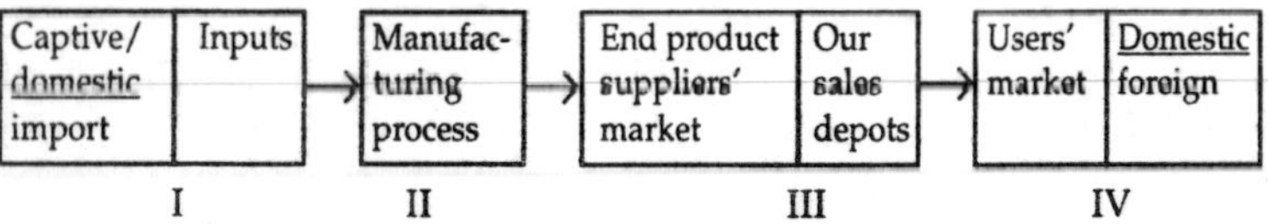

Various challenges stage-wise are as follows:

Stage I

(i) Strict observance of quality specification within permissible limits

(ii) Planned and timely supply of raw-materials

Stage II

(i) Improving quality of operation

(ii) Quality in maintenance areas

(iii) Optimising cost of manufacture

(iv) Produce more quality products in order to bring down the cost ultimately

Stage III

(i) Catering upto the level expected from us as suppliers

(ii) Aggressively emotional approach of the sales depot level with ultimate objective of "over competition"

(iii) Cent per cent fulfilment of commitment

Stage IV

(i) *Domestic*

- (a) Competitive consumer pricing
- (b) Undisruptive marketing
- (c) Updating as per customer's needs
- (d) Right type of products at right time
- (e) To reach the lowest rung of customers

(ii) *Foreign*

- (a) Competitive international pricing
- (b) Consistency in quality consumer items
- (c) Steady penetration into vital areas like production instead of maintenance

Measures for Improvements

In evinces from above that the meaning of the word' quality' differs depending on the sense it is used for and includes:

(i) Consumer preference i.e. the degree to which a specific product is preferred by the customer;

(ii) Quality of conformance i.e. the degree to which the characteristics of a product conforms to the specifications.

We are concerned about both in order to satisfy consumer preference the following steps are to be taken:

(a) Getting the standards and specifications of product on the basis of consumer's preference vis-a-vis the cost of manufacturer;

(b) Establishing a scientific inspection plan i.e. selecting and/or designing measuring instruments at different points of inspection and adopting techniques like sorting, sampling, ultrasonic testing destructive analysis etc. so that the rejected lot can be brought back to the production cycles instead of going to the despatch end.

Our main customers are domestic users and foreign users. Ours is too small a home market to sustain technical advance. It is beyond question that all of us have to look to the world as our market. Whether we compete or not is not a choice we have make. Increasing our presence and competitive capability are necessary. To do this we need a long-term strategy, a lot of commitment, a lot of determination.

In order to satisfy the users the following steps will play major role in future:

(i) To produce value-added goods our top priority needs to be quality of products and second priority is marketing strategy which is seldom discussed;

(ii) Technical collaborations will help to get internationally accepted quality of value-added goods. The terms and conditions between the licensor and licensee should be beneficial economically and acceptable;

(iii) Marketing strategy of value added goods means (a) complete understanding of the market; (b) quality; (c) price; (d) performance requirement; (e) after sale service; (f) appearance; (g) user's emotional preferences.

We of the supplier's or the seller's end are expected to follow:

(i) Mode of selling and distribution procedure followed directly or indirectly in foreign market should commensurate with the value-system prevailing in that geographical area;

(ii) Marketing segmentation being an important decision as Indian goods can be sold in some countries but not in other countries;

(iii) Once an implementation programme is fixed it should be followed in a long term basis even with a very slight benefit at the beginning because penetrating into a new market is often very costly.

As regards achieving quality conference not only the judicious selection of the basic process of manufacture is required but also careful disposal of reject materials/scraps is necessary. The latter may appear small quantity-wise but post-sale rarely gives equal return of the total cost invested for such produce which has gone to scraps. Conscious effort to be made to use them by reworking e.g. foundry scrap and other metal scrap can be used as raw materials for casting. Salvage systems, therefore, to be evolved, purely based on ultimate economic considerations.

In the human front quality circle has successfully been adopted not only as a tool for workers' development but also to increase the per capita productivity. It also let the worker see what he is doing is not only self-fulfilling but also involves him in work systems. Quality circle is not a replacement of regular quality control department. Prerequisites for successful quality circle operation are:

(i) Its members must be trained in basic techniques of problem analysis and leadership;

(ii) Top management support;

(iii) Actual implementation to precede by a careful planning ensuring maximum return.

Success can be sustained through:

(a) Regular follow-up on quality circle projects by constant appraisal and recognition (in both monetary and non-monetary forms) for work done whether implemented or not implemented.

(b) Labour-management cooperation (especially the positive reaction of the trade union leaders).

The test for measuring success of any quality circle are:

(i) improvement of quality;

(ii) saving of costs;

(iii) positive attitudinal change of workers towards work.

Postscript

Group consciousness and sense of agreeing on shared goals is of pivotal importance i.e. to make the group successful with the belief that benefit as individuals can be enjoyed later from the success of the group.

Further, an average employee is required to show a punctiliousness and attention to detail in everyday routine works much more beyond anything we find in most other industrial societies.

24

Towards Improved Statistical Era

An Essay

Prelude

For any socio-technological activity the root is man. We are all condemned to a society which is already in a statistical era, which is abundant with information, where things move very fast. And information is power. The sword or the money do not wield so much power as information do. But only jamming of information through network, media, computers is not sufficient for development. This is where statistics come in. Statistics is derived from Latin word 'status' meaning 'state'. Statistics meant mass of data relating to state. Today calculations and qualifications have pervaded all spheres. This is the age of facts, figures and statistics. Vital data matters more than the trivial. Unless the data gets exercised fast and frequently used it has only storage value.

Strength

Bernard M Baruch said, "Two lessons that experience has taught me are: getting the facts of a situation before acting is of crucial importance, and that getting these facts is a continuous job which requires eternal vigilance".

Pierre Simon Laplace, was the first to formulate the concept of 'average man' (l 'homme moyen') which is of fundamental significance in socio-economical, psycho-physiological and any kind of empirical studies related to man.

Only statistics can make sound inferences in the face of uncertainty.

The technique of control are necessary to enable the management or government to hold the higher performance level in an economic manner. Statistical control has become a science and a technology in its merit.

If decisions are not based on sound statistical grounding and optimisation, such decisions may either be 'delayed decision' or 'defective decision'.

Decisions are rescued from the cloudy realm of traditional methods into the regions of light and logic.

There are several thousand millions of activities are going on in the system whether it is government machinery, organisation etc. Any attempt to contain all kinds of transactions is futile and only statistical methods provide powerful tools.

The statistical principle of the 'vital few' is used in inventory control and quality control as "ABC Analysis" and 'Pareto Analysis' respectively.

Weaknesses

A statistician has a natural tendency for analysis, presentation and discussion of the significant components of any situation using the results of counting or measuring or trend pattern etc. But even today 85 per cent of decisions are supported on non-quantitative foundations such as insight, instinct, intuition, experience, commonsense etc. and the remaining 15 per cent are governed by the calculus of objective quantitative facts.

The opinion of people acquainted with the high level conduct of affairs is that the large majority of decisions are reached without much use of quantitative analysis or the methods of numerical analysis.

Statistics in wrong hands may turn to distortion of facts but may also become a tool of personal aggrandisement. When statistics is misused by interested parties it is said to be 'lies'.

Statistical thinking need not disperse from the mass of data and the differences within this mass. If it does to becomes unreliable and impractical.

Thoughtless and indiscriminate application of the individual item of results is against the principle of statistical thinking.

Aggregates with pejorative meanings may be harmful if highlighted for personal aggrandizement.

Sometimes it has to shun away from the shell of quantitative data whenever there is a qualitative factor.

If qualitative data do not undergo meaningful conversion valid conclusions get throttled.

Certain phenomena like poverty, awareness, opinion, moral values, behaviour etc. are not amenable to statistical analysis hence careful inferences are required.

Statistical result apply to average, not to particular. So, while administering nutrients, life-saving drugs etc. differentials must be ensured.

Inadequate and faulty data collection must be reduced.

Improvements Suggested

Whenever there is generation of data there are a number of components. Some of which are relevant for specific structural requirement whereas some are not. As much is practicable the components of data must be preserved so that whenever required it can be retrieved.

The existing statistical data system is alright but not wholesome. For example the state bureau which compiles certain economic and sociological data every decade following census is an official documentary record but has only illustrative status. It should be more detailed.

There should be nodal links to probe deeper into the specifics. For example the numerical indication of population when probed should also indicate the kinds of population, their age-mix, living standards, mortality among males and females etc. In other words the statistical gap between specific to general and general to specific to be exhaustively filled up.

The distribution patterns based on statistical figures and the basic knowledge to handle should boil down to grassroot operation level. Collection of data by field workers and review of existing structural formats may reduce the avoidable gaps.

One misconception of sampling method prevalent among administrators and economists is that to be adequate a sizeable proportion of the whole—say only 10 per cent must be in a good sample. This is incorrect. The precision of an estimate depends on the size of the sample and not on what proportion it is of the total.

Operations research, quantitative economics (econometrics), sociometry are to be developed because all these provide an analytical and objective basis for decision.

Studying only samples is inadequate. More encouragement and budget be earmarked for studying mass-data of reasonable size.

Approximation, averages, probabilities, should speak the empirical truth instead of political overtones. Right man at right time and place stating statistical figures carry lots of weight than others using statistics for self aggrandizement.

A citizen has to understand the implications and significance of statistics he comes across.

Effective Implementation Strategy

Herbert George Wells (1866-1996), celebrated thinker and writer said, "statistical thinking will be one day as necessary for efficient citizenship as the ability to read and write".

No matter how well suited to the needs of today expectations the existing utility of statistics must be reviewed as the business changes.

The idea behind any strategy comprises three questions:

- What is our activity/business?
- What should it be?
- What will it have to be?

Handling statistics is basically doing 'knowledge work', it is not only doing successfully but doing which will lead to major results. It is important to abandon what is no longer productive (or lacks utility) and to concentrate only on those scarce resources where the results are. Knowledge work is productive only when done by people of extraordinary ability. Outstanding people, however, are as scarce in knowledge work as in any other area of human endeavour.

Every knowledge, statistical or otherwise becomes obsolete. A question comes up: what else do we need? Do we need something different? Knowledge analyse is to be fed to market analysis and conclusions of market analysis to be projected to the knowledge analysis to bring out needs for new or changed knowledge.

It is no longer advisable to make data a trade secret for possible manipulation. In this open world data is open and flows. Any data gap may be uneconomical and disastrous.

The interlinking of components of any particular data are myriad by nature as in census, flora, psephology, curricula vitae etc. so at the unit level as much as possible data should be collected and arranged in general structures so that it can be retrieved.

A diagnostic approach to identify delay, time lag, idle machine hour, holding of data etc. is required. A battery of powerful statistical technique are available in the testing of diagnosis and in achieving higher level of performance.

The goals of management, whether in government on in business are of two kinds:

(a) To achieve breakthrough i.e. to create new, significant and desirable change;

(b) To achieve control i.e. to prevent any significant change from accepted standards.

These two appear to be conflicting. Unless these two qualities are there in the decision-maker it becomes impossible to activise. So is true for any management of statistical tool.

Computer utilisation time to be increased. Periodicity of data processing whenever exclusively required to be defined, in addition to 'continuous data processing'. We know how many computers have machine utilisation of 100 per cent.

Only through proper dissemination the prospect of International Information Utility (IIU) is opened up which could act as a gigantic nervous system for the entire globe and make the complete store of human knowledge instantaneously available to any human being.

Acid test of dissemination is preventing calamities like flood, storm etc. in order to save precious human life. Dissemination is successful if and only if the information networking is full-proof and communicable at microlevel.

Simple solutions need not be overlooked as solutions are not complex always.

Doctrines have their own wear and tear; and therefore they require reexamination regularly.

Computer power should be a sharable resource.

For the correct solution of any statistical problem it is not enough to collect facts with maximum accuracy but it is essential to have appropriate units employed to collect data.

Facts must be presented in a definite form not as a political circumlocution.

Ethical standards for statistical enquiry, delivery and dissemination to be framed.

25

Public Relations

A Primer

Introduction

Over the decades there have been proliferation of attempts to define Public Relations, and most of these definitions have been long and wordy. Instead of adding to this long list it's necessary to describe what I believe to be the current concept of PR practice. P.R. operates in every sphere of life; Govt. (local, regional, national, international). Business and industries (small, medium, large and transnational), community and social affairs, educational institutions, hospital and health care, charities, international affairs etc. PR theory and philosophy exists in every country, in every facet of business and private life. The emphasis, however, varies considerably according to circumstances and situations. In different countries PR practice is influenced, naturally of course, by the country's culture, religion and all other inherent characteristics.

Definitions

PR cannot operate in a Vacuum, it must be an integral part of the environment. The term PR is neither advertising, nor the 'big-boss image building, nor lobbying at the seats of power as perhaps commonly assumed. A simple definition can be "PR practice is the encouragement of harmonisation with the environment". The real role of PR, however, is "effective communication" with the community at large—be it govt. or its agencies, professional or nonprofessional bodies, intelligentsia or illiterate, consumer, industrial producer or their employees, mass media, press, opinion leaders, legislators and the like. In this regard it is appropriate to quote the declaration in the First World Assembly of Public Relations Associations: "Public Relations Practice is the art and social science of analysing trends, predicting their consequences, counselling organisation—leaders and implementing planned programmes which will serve both the organisational and public interest".

PR in India

PR, as a management tool came into vogue in India after World War-II and particularly in post-independent period. Military information units which disseminated news and information from war front were absorbed within the newly created department of public information, both at central and state level. PR activities were given a fillip by those industrial houses who operated during pre and post independent India. During this period many companies sought to get some publicity in the newspapers, often about their top people and sometimes about the events pertaining to their companies. When many companies evolved as public limited companies with large employee force and there was a need for some suitable internal communications eventually popularising the in house journals thus PR emerged as a management discipline. The managements were more and more conscious of and responsive to public attitude and public opinion. Emergence of public sector undertakings and Govt.'s policy of imposing control and directing the economy towards socialistic pattern gave a different footing to PR. PR was thus concerned about the target audience like employees, shareholders, govt. and its different agencies, opinion leaders etc.

Chief executive is the most important PR man in any organisation and his understanding or misunderstanding or PR percolates down the hierarchy. It was in this context that over the years many abuses crept into the image of PR. Despite the various vissitudes, abuses, distortions PR has survived to stay as a management tool.

In 1958 a PR society was established in India and a code of Ethics for PR was formulated. It was recognised by the International Public Relation Association. In 1968 the code of ethics was adopted. For PR practitioners quoted below are some of the "Don'ts":

(a) Sub-ordinating truth to other requirements;

(b) Circulating information not based on established and ascertainable facts;

(c) Participating in any venture unethical or dishonest or capable of impairing human dignity and integrity;

(d) Using manipulative methods so designed that individuals cannot control his own freewill and cannot be held accountable for the actions taken on them.

Philip Lesly said "PR is an organisation's efforts to facilitate the cooperation of groups of people. PR helps an organisation and its publics adopt mutually to each other". Needless to say, PR has a deliberate and integrated strategy like any other function within the organisation to contribute towards organisational objectives. PR practitioner, views the society as an organism born of the interaction among large numbers of similar and dissimilar groups both overtly or covertly. It is a relationship of interdependence. Mostly it is a relationship of unequal interdependence. One group or combination of groups dominates over the others. Often this relationship is concealed behind a facade of equality. Each of this society is held together by a community of interests real and perceived. When this community of interests disappears or no longer perceived as real the equilibrium is disturbed. The inner contradictions and tensions no longer can be contained. Upheavals and changes in the social systems takes place. In this interaction between the forces of status quo and change, of disequilibrium and equilibrium, and in the ultimate process of change itself PR communication and mass media play a very crucial role. It is true, of any small, industrial target society as well as to the global situations.

Jacques Coup de Frejac, President, of French Information Dept.. (Information et Enterprise, France) has chosen the seven pillars of PR efficiency:

1. *Shyless Combativeness:* Be offensive, knowing that it is more difficult to declare peace than to declare war. Shaking loose the inferiority complex of management, if any;
2. *Rigorous Discrimination:* Inflation of information to be deflated, unscrupulously otherwise it may eat away the vitals;
3. *Quest for Dialogue:* To speak and write and irresistible temptations. Forcible information—feeding forbids communication. After listening only one knows what one should say. A dialogue therefore is necessary;
4. *Astute Farsightedness:* To look into the past as well as into the future so risk of error can be minimised in a changing economy;
5. *Creative Research:* Off-routine careful public mapping to be researched so that the target mass is catered with the desirable inputs;
6. *Plausible Semantics:* PR semantics and wordings are to be in harmony with the understanding of our listeners. Observation and reliability are essential;
7. *Intelligence:* Intelligence means capacity to understand, power to reach general ideas, action to penetrate the mind, ability to choose the means to reach an objective, communication with people. Those comprise the nucleus of PR. PR men to be a little more intelligent than others.

Need of the Day

The relationship between the Govt., management and the ordinary people have undergone a sea-change. Politicians have realised that there is no substitute for management and whatever may be their affiiiation they tend to realise that without good management nothing worthwhile will happen. PR man has to update himself matching with changing environment reflecting new ideology PR.

Qualitative duration of PR Strategy is required to change and for affective PR the exchange of ideas shouldn't be treated as a grafting operation but is an input for widening our resource bank of creative and logical skills.

Professional skills are to cement relations between groups of people rather than the factors which divide people.

PR men are to be careful in covering the media and not be used by the Frankenstein of mass media. The objective should be to humanise media output.

PR is understood as an operational concept of management, PR is everybody's responsibility—from prime minister or chief executive downward to a clerk or a messenger.

Lastly as a specialised staff function PR is a dynamic one and continual practice will usher in a PR age.

26

Uncommon Write-up on Success

Success and failure are very common matter of life. Interestingly when we succeed we attribute our success to internal and personal factors like ability, effort, sacrifice etc. but failures are attributed quickly to external factors like other's resistance, bad luck, lacunae to task itself etc.

Each of us has a 'self-serving bias'. It operates when it is not very clear as to what actually led to a particular outcome. This is why most of us own the success but disown the failure. However, some don't claim credit for each of success nor deny responsibility for each failure.

Self-serving bias protects or boosts self-esteem and public image in general but there are some who maintain low self-esteem by not thinking very high of themselves. Such people, in fact, attribute their successes to external factors and failures to internal.

The attributes we make for our success or failure do affect our performance. He who puts his failure to his own internal inadequacy and think failure to be inevitable should start attributing to temporary external factors instead. This will improve his performance.

A pessimistic outlook is a self-destructive psychological trap. To get rid of it is the recognise that one is in it and then to stop thinking in that debilitating, unproductive way.

Seneca said way back in 58 AD, "First we must seek what it is that we are aiming at, then we must look about for the road by which we can reach it most quickly". Even those who are most successful need remainders and fresh articulations of truth; they also need to rethink, redefine, refocus and strive for excellence.

Tom Morris offers 7 practical and basic concepts which are sine qua non for meeting such challenges like finding universal conditions that guarantee success. His 7 Cs work if embodied, used, lived, and integrated into our lives at the most fundamental level of habit:

- Clear conception
- Confidence
- Concentration (focussed)
- Consistency (stubborn)
- Commitment (emotional)
- Character (good)
- Capacity (to enjoy the process)

Morris further says that the kind of success available to every human being only means using one's talent, following one's heart; and not equating wealth, fame, power or high social status. He also emphasises on equating wealth, fame, power or high social status. He also emphasises on:

- Power of imaginative vision
- Self-talk
- Inner self remainders
- Envisioning goals
- Persistence

27

Trade Union Rivalry

Causes and Nuances

Prologue

The root is man. It is not possible to say anything meaningful about the governance of man without talking about the political behaviour of man—his acts, goals, drives, feelings, beliefs, commitments, affiliations and values. Despite the cliche, man is not a political animal by nature. If he is, he is only partly so. Man's political behaviour and relations are only part of his existence as a total human being, yet they are easily absracted from the more comprehensive social environment. For some of the purposes of political analysis, this is both legitimate and necessary. Not all of man's manifold social relations are politically relevant, but enough are to suggest that we pay attention to the social matrix of political behaviour. Political man, unlike some other models of man, is not an abstraction, but socially related to other men in a variety of ways that make him a total human being. The analysis of political behaviour can best proceed, therefore, by locating man as a political actor in the social matrix of interpersonal relations. In this context it shouldn't be overlooked that behaviour is a series of acts through which man moves in time and space. Ironically the root is man and the goal too is men because studying any phenomenon related to human dynamics the target has to be an individual.

"Man is condemned to exist", said Joan Paul Sartre and Karl Marx advocated that political action is the fundamental and supreme weapon of the working class and this consciousness among working class led to 'unions' subordinate to political parties.

The close links between political parties and trade unions is a common phenomenon in developing and developed countries. In a developing country political party is a source of strength to the trade unions for the achievement of economic demands; whereas in developed countries the organised strength of trade unions influences the govt. in deciding economic issues.

Definition of Trade Union

Sidney and Beatoica Webbs define at as "a continuous association of wage-earners from the purpose of maintaining or improving the conditions of their lives" (History of Trade Unionism, London—1913).

As per Trade Union Act 1926 "trade union" means any combination whether temporary or permanent formed primarily for the purpose of regulating the relations between workmen and employers or between workmen and workmen or between employers and employers, or for imposing restrictive conditions on the conduct of any trade or businesses, and includes any federation of two or more trade unions".

A trade union is said to be active only if it is submitting correct returns to the Registrar of Trade Unions Under Section 28 of the Trade Union Act 1926.

After independence every major political party tried to control the trade unions for their self interest. They utilised trade union forum for their political base.

Trade unions are fundamentally democratic institutions and under law they are supposed to elect their office bearers every year or as per the provision of their bye-laws accepted by the Registrar of Trade Unions but often trade unions led by outside as its President/Secretary continue to have the same set of office-bearers for decades till they are either driven but by the insiders for the alleged malpractice or otherwise or until adverse circumstances acted against them to leave the profession. In Orissa although 86 per cent of the registered trade unions are run by outsiders it is seen that the remaining trade unions run by insiders are more democratic. Prolonged outside leadership without interruptions sometimes give the impression of authoritarian leadership.

Like other states outside trade union leaders of Orissa and honorary leaders. But the question remains unanswered how these honorary leaders maintain their livelihood (some of the full time trade union leaders in Orissa maintain a good standard of living) without any side-source of earning, although there is no legal restriction to get salary and allowance from the central fund account of the union.

Rivalry

Trade unions of Orissa are more or less political. Political parties are responsible for the inception, organisation, functioning and growth of trade unions. Politicalisation of Trade unions has its good and adverse effects like a flood. When the flood comes and spreads on the land it raises fertility on one hand and damages crops and cattles on the other. Likewise political trade unionism affects more adversely than the good it does to the trade union movement.

The adverse effects of the political unionism are inter-union rivalry and intra-union rivalry causing violent clashes and sabotages.

1. Inter-union Rivalry

Inter-union rivalry affects the industrial relations (IR):

(a) Separate character of demands on common issues (solutions are difficult to reach);

(b) Trial of strength by different unions by serving strike notices on different dates to show of their strengths individually. Recognition of trade union under code of Discipline in Industry to identity the sole bargaining agent in the process of collective bargaining. Such recognition is often infractous due to controversies and contradictions particularly in the industries where there is multiplicity of trade unions. In the Code of Discipline in Industry (Annexure-I) recognition is granted for a specific period hence just before the recognition period expires there is demonstration of strength by unions through violent mass-agitation, strikes, etc.;

(c) Even during the period of recognition of one union, the other union defends, liberal against it especially when it enters any agreement with the management either in its interest or against the interest of workers;

After the expiry of recognition of the particular union other union go on demanding in fresh verification shaking the industrial harmony;

(d) *Change of Party:* After verification of strength where there is change of party in power the inter-union rivalry becomes acute. So long the recognised union enjoys the confidence of party in power, it enjoys the benefit of recognition but after the change both workers and leaders become restive to change the recognised union;

(e) *Union Politics and Management Politics:* The political forces in the wider society often influence the relations between workers and unions on the one hand and management on the other. When the political preferences are opposed to each other inter-union rivalry becomes acute.

Managements purportedly do keep the party in power in good honour as a result demands of workers are not conceded to by managements and failure reports are sent by conciliation machineries and referred for adjudication involving long time. Even if it gives an award management prefers to appeal in higher courts. This disrupts industrial harmony. Sometimes to defunct a militant union managements purportedly invite outside political leaders to form union to counter militancy. Soft corner towards minor unions (with minimal followers) by managements do cause discontentment, misunderstanding and misgivings and this happens because some managements do not like to have a strong bargaining agent thus try to pamper a weak agent by encouraging multiplicity of unions to shroud the industrial environment in total confusion.

Inter-union rivalry tends to distort and polarise union views and makes them unamenable to saner counsel.

2. Intra-Union Rivlary

Intra-union rivlary i.e. the rivalry between the different interests groups within the union itself is a more recent phenomenon than inter-union rivalry:

(a) This intermecine trend emerged commensurating with the intra political rivalry in pre-independence India since 1928.

(b) It is also seen that certain unions try to capture whichever party comes to power and under its political patronage tries to survive but sentiments of militant workers are often ventilated through reports of infighting.

(b) Clashes have been reported even on conciliation table itself immediately outside the office.

(d) During the period of intra-union rivalry, both the groups submit two sets of demands to I.R. agencies and all submit two sets of return to Registrar of Trade Unions. Way back in 1954 Oscar Oranti predicted that in future trade unionism would be marked by rivalry, alliances, counter-alliances and reorganisation work.

(e) In Orissa intra-union rivalry is the intra-party factionalism. The major political parties namely Congress and Janta control the vast segment of trade unions in Orissa and political leaders of these parties frequently change colour and become power mongers. These quick shifting loyalty and ideologies bring unfair trade unionism like intra-union rivalry.

Epilogue

Keeping in view the various nuances of trade unionism it is suggested to take the following measure for a harmonious industrial set up:

(i) Multiplicity of unions to be curbed;

(ii) Regulation of political infiltration and intra-union rivalries;

(iii) The abide by the suggestion of National Commission on Labour (1960) that no union office bearer should hold office in a political party;

(iv) To ban the audit of accounts of the unions by politicians;

(v) To make trade union leaders as officially paid leaders so that members know how much they get for their service rendered; members will be careful in selecting their leaders;

(vi) When socio-political environment is chaotic, intolerant or extremist, admittedly union attitudes are unlikely to be exempt. Managements at this juncture are required to strengthen their relationship with the union by respecting the principle of mutual individuality challenge adverse environmental factors;

(vii) Mangers should leave their unions philosophy alone as a non-negotiable area and focus on the principles of their common work;

(viii) The tactical scheming of weakening the union for running the organisation better (union-baiting) the result is anti-thesis of a genuine relationship. Managements need focus not on end results they want to get out of the union but on the process both are engaged in, for in this relationship-process lies the clue to the strength of harmony and peace.

If workers are important, so is their representative group. It is vitally important that the management has a long-term perspective of the group and has a strategy for a rewarding relationship.

ANNEXURE—I

Code of Discipline in Industry

(Government of India, Ministry of Labour, Employment and Rehabilitation, Report of the National Commission on Labour, 1969)

1. To maintain discipline in industry (both in public and private sectors) there has to be: (i) a just recognition by employers and workers of the rights and responsibilities of either party,

as defined by the laws and agreements including bipartite and tripartite agreements arrived at all levels from time to time; and (ii) a proper and willing discharge by either party of its obligations consequent on such recognition.

The Central and State Governments, on their part, will arrange to examine and set right any shortcomings in the machinery they constitute for the administration of labour laws.

To ensure better discipline in industry.

2. *Management and union(s) agrees:*

(i) that no unilateral action should be taken in connection with any industrial matter and that disputes should be settled at appropriate levels;

(ii) that the existing machinery for settlement of disputes should be utilised with the utmost expedition;

(iii) that there should be no strike or lockout without notice;

(iv) that affirming their faith in democratic principles, they bind themselves to settle all future differences, disputes and grievances by mutual negotiation, conciliation and voluntary arbitration;

(v) that neither party will have recourse for (a) coercion; (b) intimidation; (c) victimisation, or go-slow;

(vi) that they will avoid: (a) litigation; (b) sit-down and stay-in-strikes; and (c) lockouts;

(vii) they will promote constructive cooperation between their representatives at all levels and as between workers themselves and abide by the spirit of agreements mutually entered into;

(viii) that they will establish upon a mutually agreed basis, a grievance procedure which will ensure a speedy and full investigation leading to settlement;

(ix) that they will abide by various stages in the grievance procedure and take no arbitrary section which would bypass this procedure; and

(*x*) that they will educate the management personnel and workers regarding their obligations to each other.

3. *Management agree:*

(*i*) not to increase workloads unless agreed upon or settled otherwise;

(*ii*) not to support or encourage any unfair labour practices such as: (a) interference with the right of employees to enrol or continue as union members; (b) discrimination, restraint or coercion against any employee because of recognised activity of trade unions; and (c) victimisation of any employee and abuse of authority in any form;

(*iii*) to take prompt action for: (a) settlement of grievances; and (b) implementation of settlements, awards, decisions;

(*iv*) to display in conspicuous places in the undertaking the provisions of this Code in local languages;

(*v*) to distinguish between actions justifying immediate discharge and those where discharge must be preceded by a warning, reprimand, suspension or some other form of disciplinary action and to arrange that all such disciplinary action should be subject to an appeal through normal grievance procedure;

(*vi*) to take appropriate disciplinary action against its officers and members in cases whose enquiries reveal that they were responsible for precipitate action by workers leading to indiscipline; and

(*vii*) to recognise the union in accordance with the criteria (evolved at the 16th session of the Indian Labour Conference held in May 1958).

4. *Union(s) agree:*

(*i*) not to engage in any form of physical duress;

(*ii*) not to permit demonstration which are not peaceful and not to permit rowdyism in demonstration;

(*iii*) that their members will not engage or cause other employees to engage in any union activity during working hours, unless as provided for by law, agreement or practice;

(*iv*) to discharge unfair labour practices, such as: (a) negligence of duty; (b) careless operation; (c) damage to property; (d) interference with or disturbance to normal work; and (e) insubordination;

(*v*) to take prompt action to implement awards, agreements, settlements and decisions;

(*vi*) to display in conspicuous places in the union offices, the provisions of the Code in the local language(s); and

(*vii*) to express disapproval and to take appropriate action against office-bearers and members for indulging in action against the spirit of this code.

28

Environmental Activity Desiderata

Preamble

Presentation of a desideratum doesn't imply that the necessary environment lacks the recommended features rather the desiderata also serve as a concept package for the empiric evaluation of actual status as a step towards improvement attempts so that the capacity is upgraded to protect the environment we live in.

Earth in the Balance

Environmental conservation has been the most talked about thing these days. The awareness has reached the present stage over the past 40 years. The root of the problem is violence, the latent instinct in men which has reflected in many ways viz. abuse of basic human rights, lack of genuine concern for the poor, social and political strife, racial and religious intolerance, armament and gun factories etc.

Arnold J. Toynbee's apt remark is relevant in this context. He said, "Technology is the magic that grinds out wealth and power and human beings rush to buy wealth and power at any price." Technology "at almost any price" is surely going to affect the nature. It is essential to strike a balance between technology and conservation, a balance between material aspiration and spiritual. If adequate care is not taken then further degradation shall take place which will only be precursor to spiritual and cultural death of India or any country whatsoever.

Human life and work can not be thought of without an environment. The physical, chemical, biological, social, psychological, factors in environment play an important role in the normal functioning of man. When these factors exceed certain limiting values there occurs undesirable effect in the basic living of man. Reciprocally man too is an environmental factor with respect to other members of an eco-system.

By-products of industry, use of chemicals against pests, mosquitoes, removal of overburden of mining etc. may appear to be against environment but in favour of economic progress; therefore what is called for is a responsible management of earth's resources, striking a right balance between conservation and development.

We are all concerned with the question whether (or perhaps when) man must design and adapt to steady state conditions (with maximum ability to resist perturbations) and at the same time avoid the ageing state. In the short history of man-on-earth there has been succession of growth states and now that there might be "limits to growth" in man's world is a new, and, to many people, almost unthinkable.

Mankind can do almost anything he puts his mind, to provided he does not break natural laws in the process. Man must overcome his belief of being dominant over nature. He needs to work with the nature's forces rather than against them. Technology supplies the tools but it is man who has to apply these tools for the benefit of environment and his future.

It is necessary for us, as the wise custodian of this frail earth, to recount how our ocean and atmosphere came into being. Berkner and Marshal have described that it is not by men but by micro-organisms. Over long periods of time, have largely controlled the chemical compositions of the sea, likewise for the atmosphere. The earth's original atmosphere, as derived from purely geological processes, contained little or no Oxygen and much Carbon dioxide until green plants began realising the former and removing the latter. As a dependent heterotroph (means nourished by others in contrast to autotroph which means self-nourishing) man can't alone control the bio-sphere for his own good; he must have the cooperation of the micro-organisms of the soil and water, bacteria, other autotrophs and many other organisms. Organisms, which are mostly invisible, work for the good of man and nature; these are adaptable, tough and composed of living protoplasm vulnerable to poisons as man himself. Too often man works to obtain temporary advantage by increasing flow of materials but forgets to arrange for return mechanism by branding as uneconomical.

Bionomics

A change in public attitude towards the environment begin first in the affluent countries but is now slowly spreading to the less developed countries as political leaders began to realise that it is in the best interest of each country, large and small, be concerned with the big picture as well as with internal problems.

Environmental principles contribute to achieving a mature balance between the systems of man and the systems of the nature in such a way that quality controls and quantity and human values are not sacrificed on the alter of technological advancement. Integration of man and nature is of crucial significance. Integration is much more than a sum of the parts. It should not be forgotten that mere sum of trees does not make a forest.

Beneficial use of resources is the net benefit of "good" resources (environment-friendly) and "bad" resources (pollutants). Bionomics is a kind of expanded economics that includes cost accounting of the works of nature as well as the works of man. Literally bionomics mean "management of life" is derived from the same root (nomic; management) as economics (basically means management of the house).

Pollutant So Many

Many economically important human activities emit gaseous pollutants into the air. Some of these are highly stable and continue to reside in the atmosphere for decades, even centuries e.g.

Name	Residence (in years)	Annual Growth Rate (in %)
Carbon dioxide	3	0.50
Nitrous oxide	150	0.25
Methane	11	1.00
Chloro fluoro carbon (CFC-11)	75	7.00
Chloro flouro carbon (CFC-12)	111	7.00
CFC-13	90	17.00
Halon-1301	110	20.00

Every molecule of CFC warms up the global temperature 10,000 times more than a molecule of Carbon dioxide. USA, Canada, Norway, Sweden etc. have banned the use of CFC as these spoil the Ozone layer, damaging the "greenhouse effect" on earth. Discovery of atmospheric holes has alarmed the scientists. Halons, primarily used in the fire extinguishers, damage the Ozone layer 0.10 times more destructively than the CFC, CFC is used as refrigerator fluid since 1928.

The word "pollution" is derived from a Greek root meaning defilement. Preston Cloud defined pollution as an undesirable change in the physical, chemical or biological characteristic of air, water or land that will be, or may be harmful to human and other life, industrial processes, living conditions and cultural assets.

A. Effects of Air Pollution

1. Impairs physical properties of atmosphere by adversely affecting its visibility, transparency and precipitating the cloud due to hygroscopic nature of pollutant materials;
2. Damages through abrasion, chemical attack, indirect chemical attack and electro-chemical abrasion;
3. Visible and invisible impact on vegetation like stunted growth, morphological pigmentation;
4. Increases mortality among domestic and livestock animals;

5. For human beings air is essential for the sense functions. One can live without food for 5 weeks, without water for 5 days but without air for only 5 minutes.

B. Effects of Water Pollution

Environmental Protection Agency (EPA) under National Interest Primary Drinking Water Regulations (1975) has classified the various water pollutants and their maximum permissible level:

	Water Pollutant	Maximum Permissible Level (mg. per litre)
1.	Inorganic chemicals	
	Arsenic	0.05
	Barium	1.00
	Chromium	0.05
	Fluoride	1.40 to 2.40
	Lead	0.05
	Mercury	0.002
	Nitrate	10.00
	Silver	0.05
2.	Organic chemicals:	
	Endrin	0.0002
	Methoxychlor	0.10
3.	Radioactivity (Pico-Curie unit per litre):	
	Gross Alpha	15.0
	Radium 226, 228	5.0
	Tritium	20.000
	Strontium-90	8.0
4.	Bacteriological	
	Coliform Bacteria per 100 ml	1.0

C. Effects of Sound Pollution

According to the International standards the noise level should not exceed 45 decibels (dB). Beyond permissible limits noise too have harmful effects like hormonal imbalance, migraine, fatigue, psychic disorders etc.

Based on laboratory data scientists have discovered the following effects on the human beings:

- 50dB-Comfortable hearing
- 80-90dB-Headache
- muscular fatigue
- blood vessel contraction
- increases heartbeat
- 90-100dB-Impairment of visibility and hearing
- 100-140 dB-Memory loss, madness
- 155 dB-Wrinkles, ageing
- 180 dB-Death.

D. Effects of Mining Activities

The basic complaints of environmentalists against open cast mining are that such mining:

1. Disfigures the landscape not only by excavation but by creating huge dumps of vegetation and overburden;
2. Pollute the atmosphere with dust and noise;
3. Contaminates the ground as well as the surface water caused by effluent tailing ponds;
4. Destroys forests, thereby causing disappearance of birds and wildlife from their natural habitat to elsewhere;
5. Displaces native tribals who are most often the ancient residents of the forests.

E. Pollution in Mine

(a) Water Pollution

1. Effluents from ore beneficiation plants, waste dumps/ tailing lines;
2. Spent water from ore handling plant;
3. Removal of accumulated more water often toxicated by explosive chemicals and other solids;

(b) Air Pollution

1. Mining activity linked with gaseous explosive pollutants like Sulphur dioxide, Carbon monoxide, Oxides of Nitrogen etc.;
2. Suspended materials like mineral dust Silica etc. originating from drilling, crushing, automobile, mining machinery exhausts etc.

(c) Noise Pollution

1. From fixed plant and machineries of mineral beneficiation plant, conveyors, compressors etc.;
2. From moving sources like shovels, dumpers, drills, dozers, trucks, front-end loaders;
3. From sudden noise like blasting.

F. Detergent Threat

Many detergents are made of complex chemicals which cause dermatological toxicity and are environmental threat too. The researchers at Karnataka University have inferred from a study that 80 per cent of infant skin problems were cured by avoiding detergents to wash napkins. Unsafe formulation of synthetic detergents (SYNDET) often give rise to dermal effects. Studies undertaken by Industrial Toxicology Research Centre (ITRC), Lucknow also reveal that the synthetic detergents in cloths and crockery need to be washed for clothes (20 to 23 times) and for crockery (11 to 13 times) to make them free of detergents. As per ITRC study in a detergent factory, dermatit is spread from worker's hands to other parts. Worker's exposure to related chemicals of SYNDET like caustic soda, potash, oleum, sulfuric chloro hydrin, ethylene oxide etc. also cause irritation in respiratory tract, asthma, laryngitis and allergies. The desired qualities of detergent are good detergency or washing efficiency, adequate dispersing and emulsifying properties without damage to the fabric and human beings.

The Basic Strategy

Any strategy of evolving actions towards environmental protection the following non-exhaustive points are to be kept in mind:

1. Shortage of resources to be adjusted against economic and social mal-distribution;
2. Basic human needs are: food, shelter, clothing, health and education. Any activity of development must protect the needs;
3. World statesmen are to direct the new system to match the 'Inner limits" of the basic human needs without violating the "outer limits" of the plant's resources;
4. Environmental is highly inter connected viz. people, resources, development and many others; so action to solve one issue may affect the others;
5. Environmental management is to be flexibly planned to cope with the uncertainty which many come up; as such for general development strategy alternative patterns should preferably be prepared side by side.

We must be careful with the word "stability" since it means different to different people. The physical scientist measures it in terms of resistance and perturbation i.e. a system is stable if it returns quickly to equilibrium when disturbed by an external agency. It is called structural or neighbourhood stability.

The environmental scientist sees the stability in the time-related scene i.e. a system is stable if its structure and function remain almost the same over the years.

Ultimately however the survival or the life of the system is governed by these perturbation-related of time-related fluctuations.

The natural tendency of nature is to diversify but when it reduces the energy efficiency it contradicts the current strategy of man and a conflict grows between man and nature. It becomes a matter of concern to what extent it is necessary or desirable.

A Bold Step Ahead

UNESCO in 1973-74 initiated the MAB (Man and the Biosphere) programme adopted by India in 1983.

The Indian region (8-38 N and 60-97.5 E) with a total area of 328 million hectares is rich in biological diversity. It is estimated that there are around 65,000 species of animals including mammals, around 45,000 species of plants around 15,000 species of vascular flora (vegetation cover), around 50,000 species of insects, 4,000 species of mollusks, 6,500 species of invertebrates, 2,000 kinds of fishes, 1,200 kinds of birds, 420 species of reptiles, 340 species of mammals, 140 species of amphibians.

Idea of conservation is not a new one for India. Ancient Indian literature has emphasised the conservation of flora and fauna. Above all the Ashokan edict also bears ample testimony.

This step taken by the UNESCO and our country has started bringing about good dividends through change in the psyche and creative activities like animal libraries, river and lake saving activities, love for sanctuaries, afforestation (list of trees in Indian context, Annexure-I) etc.

Basing on the standard criteria for selection by UNESCO the Indian National MAB Committee identified the following sites as protected biosphere reserves:

Reserve	State(s)
Nilgiri	Tamil Nadu, Karnataka and Kerala
Namdapha	Arunachal Pradesh
Nanda Devi	Uttar Pradesh
Northern Andamans	Andaman & Nicobar Islands
Gulf of Manor	Tamil Nadu
Kaziranga	Assam
Sunderban	West Bengal
Thar Desert	Rajasthan
Mannas	Assam
Kanha	M.P.
Nokrek	Meghalaya (Tura Range)

Projects recommendations specifying boundary, structure are management have been submitted for the above mentioned first four reserves.

Postscript

Different ways in which nations perceive their environmental problems and eventually tackle them is determined by the characteristics of their individual political system. L.J. Landquist stresses the "politicalness" of the environmental issue: "It is not by trying to get into the fields of engineers, scientists, ecologists or philosophers that we can make most important contributions. Proposals for change must be based on careful empirical analysis of the political effects of the environmental politics and policies".

Basically two models of regulation exists and their characteristics are as follows:

.*The American Model:* Emphasises adherence to standards, constant monitoring of standards, strict schedules. Public and Press keep a surveillant eye over the environment protection agency (Watch the Watch dog). Bureaucratic power is limited by standards, schedules and public litigation.

The British Model: Assumes that several constraints are faced by the political system as well as by the industry and therefore environment considerations are to be put into the proper perspective. It does not prescribe strict standards or schedules. It relies on the local implementors to arrive at "most practical and feasible solution".

In other words American model is process-oriented whereas the British model is result-oriented. Most administrative models adopted by India and other Third World Countries lie somewhere in the spectrum of American model being at extreme right and British model at extreme left. More specifically in India environmental regulations follow British pattern whereas the implementation style follows American model. As a result, our system inherits not only the strengths but also the weaknesses of both models.

There is need for a revolution in mankind's thinking as basic as the one introduced by Copernieus who first pointed out that the earth was not the centre of the Universe. For shaping the future our mind-set is to be changed i.e. the paradox of thinking obsolescence and living in rapidly changing flux is to be cleared because this paradox puts us in collision with the future. It is the responsibility of "you" and "I" to save and shape the future. Technological advances and improvements in the quality of life should be complementary to each other Technology should not merely strengthen the arms of industrialists of nation. It has a far greater role to play.

A new ethic is to be imbibed. Kiniteness of resources, life, crises, life-supporting systems etc. are to be kept in mind and from this "new political man" is to emerge. Voting regularly is not enough. Individual involvement in political and environmental issues will be essential part of the emerging new ethics.

"O Earth whatever we dig out from you, must that have to be filled up again and restored as fast as possible. O Pure One, we do not intend to hit you at your heart of hearts."

(Atharva Veda 12/1/35)

ANNEXURE—I

Names of Trees for Afforestation

Sl. No.	Common Indian Name	Botanical Name
1.	Acacia (Kikar)	Acacia Nitotica
2.	Amla	Phyllanthus Emblica
3.	Ashok (Ashok)	Polyalthia Longifolia
4.	Arjun (Arjun)	Terminalia Arjuna
5.	Bael (Bel)	Aegle Arjuna
6,	Banyan (Barh)	Ficus Benghalensis
7.	Bougainvillea (Boganvila)	Bougainvillea Spectabilis
8.	Cashewnut (Kaju)	Anacardium Occidentale
9.	Casuarina (Suru)	Casuarina Equisetifolia
10.	Chakundi	Cassia Siamia
11.	Drumstick (Saijan)	Moraiga Delifera)
12.	Eucalyptus (Safeda)	Eucalyptus Hybrid
13.	Flame of Forest (Palas)	Butea Monosperma
14.	Gambhar	Gamalina Arboria

(Contd...)

15.	Gauva (Amrud)	Psidium Gualava
16.	Gulmohar (Gulmohar)	Delonix Regia
17.	Imli	Tamrindus Indica
18.	Jackfruit (Kathal)	Artocarpus Heterophyllus
19.	Jamun	Eugenia Jambolana
20.	Jujube (Ber)	Ziziphus Mauritiana
21.	Krishnachuda	Poisiana Regia
22.	Mahua	Bissia Latifolia
23.	Neem (Neem)	Azadirachta Indica
24.	Pangam (Karanja)	Derris Indica
25.	Red Silk Cotton (Simul)	Bomfax Ceiba
26.	Sal	Shorea Vobusta
27.	Shishum (Sisso)	Dalbergia Sisso
28.	Teak	Tectona Grandis
29.	Thuja (Morpankhi)	Thuja Compacta
30.	Pipal (Pipal)	Ficus Religiosa

29

A Critical Look Into Environment

Policy and Practice

Environmental policy and practice are two different matters. Environmental policy is the sum of objectives and measures designed to regulate society's interaction with the environment as a natural system. It comprises of aspects of restoration, conservation and structural adjustment. Since society's existence ultimately depends on the natural environment and its resources, environmental policy, in principle, has to involve all societal rules governing the use of nature by human beings.

Practice does not conform to this broad definition of environmental policy. The scope is always vast, the policy laid down noble but the implementation through rigours of practice deviates from the principle due to constraints and reasons beyond control.

Till date environmental policy has been designed as "react-and-cure" strategy viz. control of air, water quality, noise abatement and waste disposal with emphasis on restoration and reclamation aspects. Such strategy is definitely meaningful and still necessary although it has its inherent deficits. To overcome such weaknesses preventive environmental policy designed on "anticipate-and-prevent" has become necessary.

Reactive environmental strategy has following shortcoming:

— it is expensive;

-- identifies relevant problems very late;

— measures adopted give late effect, often damaging eco-system;

— focuses on a small part of the problem of society environment;

— lack of coordination between measures;

— media specific (like air, water, noise, waste);

— shifting of environmental problem from one media to other or from one space to another (long range, trans-boundary);

— dilemma of principle, whether polluter pays or tax payer pays.

Preventive strategy counters these but the transition from the reactive to preventive requires research, conceptual innovations and empirical studies. Certain examples are:

— reduction of automobile emission and acceptable solutions economically sound;

— envisaging future impacts of new technology;

— priorities for action to contain forest damage.

Preventive strategy is not an easy task. It passes through complexity, uncertainties, time pressure, inadequate political will, lack of analytical method and anticipatory administrative skill etc.

Pragmatically a combination of both can be a wholesome approach towards environment. Both of them complement each other, just as they do in the practice of medicine.

Human Organism

Understanding life is not easy. Each method is true; if we define life as a chemical process then chemical method grasps a section of life. If life is a physical process, a physical method may reveal another section of life but to comprehend life as a whole these separate numerous results of sciences and humanities are to be integrated.

Human organism is a self-organising system, there is continuous adjustment going on "inside" the human being and with the environment "outside". The temperature, the water content, the chemical metabolism and other "internal conditions" are maintained at an astonishing constant level vis-a-vis the changing conditions of the "external environment" by a system of ingenious devices.

The stability of human organism has its own threshold limits before it breaks down to irreversible instability. To maintain this stability or orderliness we are required to contribute so that human life itself is conserved on this spaceship called "earth".

In the human body short-term and long-term adjustments do take place. Short term adjustments are empirically analysable but very little is known as to what occurs in human body during long term adjustments. Human organism learns over a long period of time by reacting less violently to external stimuli to come to terms placidly with external environment through what we name as "habituation". It is often misunderstood that man can come to terms with anything. Philosophical habitation of human organism has its limits. Human endurance is not limitless.

Unlike animals humans actively alter or shape their environment. This alteration of environment by man has its own problems and dangers too. There may be new kind of stresses which body can't adjust. Environmental contamination like mercury poisoning or nuclear leakage etc. cannot be adjusted.

Culture and civilisation are possible because of psycho-somatic adjustment processes in the human organisms. This adjustment is the foundation for our freedom for our self realisation as human beings on earth and without this we are reduced to non-entities. Man is consequential to his internal and external environment habituated in his existential being.

Risk Assessment Framework

Response to risk is not adequate. There is no framework for risk analysis, risk assessment, risk evaluation, and risk management. Risks are manifold:

— voluntary risks;

— risks modified by risk-takers behaviour;

— risks taken involuntarily;

— risks taken in ignorance of hazard;

— risks although awareness exists but level of hazard not known;

— short term hazards effects years later;

— procedural risks, immediate assessment not possible.

Environmental risks relate to poverty, sanitation, agro-business, industrialisation. In developed countries it is due to waste disposal, nuclear reactor leakage, drug, high potency anti-biotics, genetically manipulated products etc.

Often the "probability of harm" and "degree of benefit" are weighed and comparative edge is accepted. Hardly any effort is made to annul the harm content.

We live in a risky world and while we reduce and eliminate some risks (if not all), we also create newer and more hazardous risks. In order to survive in a risky world and make our state a welfare state we must protect "SHE", it stands for SAFETY, HEALTH & ENVIRONMENT. As individuals, as govt. as country this is our primary task. Any contamination to SHE will be alarming to mankind.

Cause and Cure

The roots of present environmental crises today are due to man's unlimited desires, greed ignorance and the materialistic approach to life. Over and above all these is rapid industrialisation based on exploitation of natural resources and side by side there is growth of population. As such there is over use of land, water and air as well as degradation of these due to dust, smoke, sewerage, industrial discharge etc. Chemical and physical contamination of water, air and soil, and also agro-product have been causing health hazards. Causes are well known but the control is inadequate. Public health and hygiene have gone out of control.

The only cure is, the individual and the nation must re-dedicate towards conservation and protection of environment before it is too late. A balance is to be maintained between material aspiration and human survival. To achieve this, curative objective the religious practices and beliefs are to be reinstilled into the mind of men so that further onslaught on nature is curbed. Developing and environmental ethics based on cultural traditions can also be thought of education content and mass media are to be made supportive.

It must not be forgotten that so long as the earth has mountains, rivers, forests the human race will survive.

30

Man, Quality of Thought and Environment

In ancient days man was defined, as a "featherless biped" (dressed chicken?). Subsequently this definition was modified to 'featherless rational biped'. Through man become *Homo sapiens* as well as *Homo faber* (the maker) through *homo erectus*. Man makes from what he thinks. He has immense possibilities in him. He is capable of discovering, inventing, altering, learning, unlearning, changing mind set and what not! The core of man is his self and his thought. Jean Paul Sartre, existential philosopher had told "I exist therefore I think". Human thought is the highest form of activity among living species in general and mankind in particular. Over the millennia it has evolved to what we are today and we can't afford to be extinct. After all we are *Homo economicus* also.

Every advancement begins in a small way within the individual man. Only man has evolved culturally to the point where he only can alter consciously and radically his physical environment and his own biological makeup. It is people who make things happen and bring changes. People need to be developed to initiate change, participate in it, facilitate it and manage it in the desired direction. However, unless there is professionalism, sometimes they become victims of their creation. Learning is coping and coping is survival.

Dr. Gillotine has rightly said that we are the victims of our own sophistications. Technological advancement must not shrink the conscience of man. Man is developmental as well as rational His rationality arises out of the quality of thought. Man is no longer confined to a region, he is a global citizen. To be an earth citizen, he is to go beyond the present frontiers of consciousness which fragments everything and also divides the outer from the inner. Developing an individual who is an integrated man, a spiritual man and a perfect man is the ultimate aim of human existence.

Toxicity in man is inherent. Beware of man who is a dis-organiser, over-busy, unprincipled person without definite objectives, offenders who hit and operate blindly, the complicators, the ever organised at the cost of unnecessary man and materials. They need corrective and therapeutic measures. For them what is required is tolerance, learning to tolerate. Unless man's action, thought and behaviour are of quality, there can't be real improvement of him and his makings. For example, today the biosphere has become the most important problem faced by man. There is ongoing replacement of the communities of nature by mandate community. But unless the principles governing the life of natural communities, are observed for the man-made communities, mankind may not thrive. We must think less about conquering nature and more about learning to work with nature. The interdependence of man with the rest of nature including his fellow human beings is of crucial significance for survival. Human activity alters landscape, atmosphere and also fellow human beings (consumers). Unless man balances the onslaughts on nature and his conscience disaster becomes imminent. Pro-action is the in-thing today than reaction. Man is becoming more and more aware of total quality thinking. Man has to become self regulatory. Through conscious effort man can achieve excellence in environment which comes as a natural corollary to high quality in living and thinking.

I, we and us matter ultimately in the survival of human species. Let me question myself as to how I can control the damage caused by me to nature on the surroundings. Can we not together increase the awareness of our neighbours for a better world, for a better future to live in? Let us do self assessment as to whether we actually, want it or not? Obvious questions to ponder are: How are we inter connected? How is the welfare of the whole is affected by the welfare of the individual? What if people could not speak freely? What if people would not share?

As an earth citizen, I feel happy to know that international agreements prohibit military or other hostile use of environmental modification techniques having widespread, long lasting or severe effects. Technologies are becoming fiscally responsible life conserving and environmentally friendly. It is no technology if it affects human life adversely in whatsoever manner.

There is de-massification of society into nuclear families, isolated communities, divorces, deserters etc. Unless man does something to protect him and his neighbour there will be no end to his fall. Let us not forget that we live at a fantastic moment of human history. Let us give a better world, less energy intensive and less polluting to our posterity.

Let there be more conscientious use of power, money and service. Man must not be carried away blindly by group process. Let him stick to simple principles, then only he can do good work, stay free from chaos, confusion, conflict and consumerism etc.

Let us not forget the fact that the potency comes for knowing what is happening and acting accordingly. Paradoxically, freedom comes from obedience to natural order. Since all creation is a whole, separateness is an illusion. Like it or not we are team players. Power comes through cooperation, independence through service and greater self through selflessness. India being a champion of spiritualism over the millennia has the potential to be a world leader in containing the issue of environmental protections and this can be achieved by you, me and us together through changing our mind-set and qualitative change in thinking.

31

A View on Open Cast Mining Through Matrix Method

Introduction

Environment comprises the atmosphere (air), water (both surface and underground), plant, land and animal habitat around us as well as the human habitation. Humanity draws from nature for its survival and progress but to be aggressive on the nature for rapid economic progress of the society has been counter-productive. Depletion of plants and animals, pollution of water and air beyond permissible limits have only brought disease and misery to mankind.

When population and industrialisation grew rapidly during last few decades, protection of environment become a matter of concern and the first legislation—Environment (Protection) Act, 1980 was enacted in our country.

Mining Activity

Mines especially open cast iron ore mines have no option as to choice of site because unlike other industries, it has to be at a site where the ore body is located at a depth underneath deep forest over million of years. To reach the ore, removal of trees and barren rocks are necessary and removal of these wastes for maintaining proper bench height amounts to 10 to 20 per cent of the volume of ore.

Felling of trees, levelling of hill-slopes, removal of waste, quarrying of ore, dumping of rejects etc. form an interlinked inseparable unit of activity which continue till the reserves last or till the demand for ore persists.

In the Keonjhar-West Singhbhum thrust zone (Bonai) there are a number of mines (mostly iron and manganese) in Barajamda-Koria region. All these mines are open cast and their mode of working are governed by Mines Act 1952 and Metalliferous Mines Regulation 1961.

As such the open cast mining activity can be broken into a number of natural and consequential elemental subactivities, which can be illustrated viz.

- shaving the earth's surface;
- changing topography;
- dislocating soil and subsoil;
- infinitesimal change of gravitational effect on air and water;
- movement of gravel, silt, slime;
- shockwaves affecting water bodies;
- pH impact of soil, water;
- migration of fauna;
- impact due to human and cattle concentration;
- emission of vehicles, machines, blasting etc.
- change in livelihood of local population;
- influx of cosmopolitan population of different habits values, cultures;
- wide range of trades and vocations;
- impact of communications services like roads, telephones;

- impact on inflation arising out of labour intensive enhanced wage;
- poor tribal survival on supply of fire-wood;
- non-availability of coal (especially in non-coal mines) and dependency on electricity for domestic energy;
- paucity of water source and supply;
- mushrooming growth of unhygienic habitation and their undesirable growth;
- breakdown of joint families;
- rootlessness in society;
- social disorders and related problems;
- growth of obstinate type of malarial parasites, dysentery, cholera, typhoid etc.

Opencast mines activity is often viewed as anti-environment because most of these mines are located in forest and this activity requires overburden removal through felling of trees; excavations while making mining roads, pits on surface caused land degredation; creation of wastedumps, slime (washouts) affecting crop, ground water etc.

In a business scenario of demand and supply, the desired grade and size of ore naturally produce some reject and in case of iron ore, the demand from user steel plants is mainly for lumps and the lump production is only 30 per cent of the total produce. The balance is fines, the utility of which at present, doesn't match the quantity produced; as a result, huge dumps of fines are created and will continue to remain till steel plants make more sinter.

It is interesting to note that total value of mineral production is a mere 2.5 per cent approx of the net national product (National Income). Further, the total area under mining lease (excl. coal) stands at 8000 sq. km which is only 0.3 per cent of total land area of country, the actual area of mining face comes to 0.05 per cent. In contradistinction, quantitatively speaking, the damage caused by concrete urbanisation, river valley hydel projects, agriculture, flood etc. much more than what is caused by mining taking the country surface as the frame of reference.

Imolesi Matrix of Impacts

E. Imolesi, Bologna (Italy) has developed a method for assessment of environmental impact of surface mining operations based on use of matrices. It is a tool for unbiased analysis of the effects during and after the industrial activity i.e. surface mining on the natural and social environment.

Environmental impact from land values induced by surface mining activities is often assessed by means of subjective evaluations which may be prone to be influenced by the personal attitude of the appraiser and the approach/angle selected by him. On the other hand, a reliable vision and prediction of the possible consequences at the planning stage would be very helpful in order to minimise the damage in different fronts.

By comparing the technical options at hand with the standard global accounting index of various environmental aspects, the most advantageous decisions can be made by the administrative authority and the engineer resulting in a correct balance of private and public interest.

This matrix method of environmental impact assessment (EIA) aims at:

- the evaluation of the global effect of a surface mining operation including not only naturalistic values (wildlife, landscapes) but also economic, social and cultural aspects related to the industrial activity in as much as all these factors concur to the improvement of the quality of life.
- providing a practical tool for decision making amongst different options at the project stage and is adopted as a standard procedure to be included within project document.
- Minimising the risk of personal judgement by the project engineer and the public administrator.

Construction of this Matrix is known as AEVIA—an Italian acronym of Attivita Estrattive Valutazione di Impatto Ambientale (means Environmental Impact Assessment of Mining Activity).

This method is based on the construction of a matrix having 41 rows and 12 columns (Table 31.1 and 31.2): its elements are algebraic values either positive or negative, if quality of life is deteriorated or improved respectively. These figures represent the data base for the overall evaluation of environmental impact.

TABLE—31.1

Sl. No.	Row	Subset Ambit	Broad Class
1.	Mineral resources	A. Earth	
2.	Morphology		
3.	Hydrography	B. Water	
4.	Hydrogeology		Physico-chemical
5.	Climatic	C. Air	
6.	Physico-chemical		
7.	Influence areas	D. Dynamics	
8.	Stability		
9.	Spontaneous	E. Flora	
10.	Cultivated		
11.	Protected species		
12.	Terrestrical	F. Fauna	Biological
13.	Aquatic		
14.	Avifauna		
15.	Protected species		
16.	Wet land and forest	G. Land utilisation	
17.	Grazing		
18.	Agricultural		
19.	Commercial		
20.	Residential		
21.	Industrial		
22.	Mining		
23.	Land preservation		
24.	Lands care	H. Protected area	Cultural, social and economic factors
25.	Parks and preserves		
26.	Hydrogeological		
27.	Historical		
28.	Military		
29.	Urban development		

30.	Cultural model	I. Cultural and social aspects
31.	Recreational activity	
32.	Employment	
33.	Driven activity	
34.	Health	
35.	Energy supply	J. Infrastructure
36.	Road network	
37.	Dumps	
38.	Local	K. Economy
39.	Regional	
40.	National	
41.	International	

TABLE—31.2

Sl. No.	Columns	Broad Class
1.	Road and excavation faces	
2.	Networks	
3.	Production rates	
4.	Plants (Beneficiation and infrastructure)	Industrial activity
5.	Transportation	
6.	Waste Dumps	
7.	Site Rehabilitation	
8.	Profitability	Social and economic aspects
9.	Production value	
10.	Investment	
11.	Nuisances	Health Safety
12.	Civil works	

Each row corresponds to a character typical of a subset ambit (eg. earth, air, flora, ... social life, culture etc. total 11 in number) belonging to 3 broads classes. Physicochemical, Biologic, cultural-economic-social. It is shown in Table—31.1.

Similarly, each of the 12 columns correspond to an elementary actions typical of mining activity shown in Table—31.2. Each of this columnar activity is capable of producing a modification of the environment.

Determination of Matrix

As explained, each row stands for an elementary characteristic and each column an elementary action.

Each element (E) of 41 x 12 matrix having 41 rows (R) and 12 columns (C) is obtained as a product of two factors:

E (XY) = R (X) x C (Y)

Where X can have value ranging from 1 to 41 and Y has value from 1 to 12.

R (X) is the weight of Yth action only on Xth characteristic taken into consideration; whereas C (Y) is a algebraic value of basic impact of Yth action the environment.

It may so happen that interference is absent when a certain characteristic is not affected at all nor altered by a given action.

The correct appraisal of the level of interference between an elementary action and a given environmental characteristic chiefly depends on:

- the original state of the environment;
- the quality and relevance of the project.

Therefore, application of matrix method becomes meaningless if the environment, where mining activity is hosted is unknown or scarcely defined, and if the project is not developed with specific professional competence in the sector.

Granted a correspondence between the qualitative level of interference and the value of each element in the matrix; the calculation of the level of impact is either high (4), medium (2), low (1) or null (0).

For computer data processing firstly the matrix of coefficient is set up representing level of interference. For each Y-th action, the average level of interference with the various characteristic of environment is calculated.

Secondly, elementary impacts are summed up by rows (characteristics) and by columns (actions) to obtain cumulative impact figures, indicating which of the various environmental characteristics is the most affected by mining activity either adversely (corresponding to highest positive value of impact element) or favourably (highest negative value).

The study of a complex system, such as mining operation and the surrounding environment can be carried out through analysis of various interferences, so that overall benefit over time can be maximised. Not only nature degradation can be regulated, controlled and prevented through rational analysis but also the quality of life of residents of an open-cast mine can be considerably improved taking the most appropriate decisions which are otherwise difficult to single out.

Concluding Cue from the Wise

Gregory Bateson's wisdom is true for most phenomena: "To connect as much as possible the unconnected, the seemingly unrelated has an invisible connection". External factors are as important as internal factors but striking a balance can only be based on rational analysis, vision into the far future and never on routine way of thinking.

32

Errors and Accidents

In spite of rapid technological progress and automation human beings still continue to be the key resources. In spite of global population growth "workers" remain to be scarce and costly resource. Man is the maker of his destiny. He is the discoverer, he is the inventor who directs his own future to higher levels of evolution. It is the brain and the brawn of the ancient worker-man who made old stone age, metal weapons followed by more recent nuclear weapons. He who works, contributes in some form or other. It is the sanctity of work that matters not the chair.

But human beings are not gods they may be replica of gods busy is small things of existence. They are prone to commit errors, even blunders which may decelerate a retard progress. When a man errs unknowingly it is a mistake, but when he errs knowingly, it is sabotage. The act of man is due to:

(i) Internal (work) stressors;

(ii) External (other than work) stressors

Cause may be either of these or a combination of both; and the effect is an "act". About 80-85 per cent of human errors are due to stressors at worksite and only 15-20 per cent are due to family pressure, stress strain. This is how the worksite, the colleagues, the environment factors (like organisation structure, job procedure, workplace design etc.) ignorance of SOP (Standard Operating Practices) SMP (Safe Maintenance Procedures), fatigue due to overwork, age etc. make man prone to commit errors.

Human errors at different echelons of organisation may result in:

(i) Active operational failures

(ii) Latent or dormant failures

Active operational failures occur due to lack of understanding signals, reflex failures to vital information, wrongful optimisation in practice. Its adverse impact is immediately resplendent in machine failures, breakdown loss of human life and machines due to accident.

Whereas dormant failures lurk secretly for a long time in the system arising only due to fallible decisions at some level or other of organisation. The damaging consequences are harmful for men, money and machines.

Human errors are the 'cause', accidents are the 'effect' of such cause. Human errors can be prevented. These errors have 'hardware' and 'software' aspects based on which the strategy for prevention can be formulated:

Hardware Strategy

- work design must confirm to ergonomics;
- SOP (Standard Operating Practices) and SMP (Safe Maintenance Procedures) must be prepared;
- Up-to-date procedure, tolerance limits to be made available;
- Introduction of defence system for containment protection, detection and escape;
- Provide infrastructure for better social and psychological;
- Marketing safety to all employees in general.

Software Strategy

- Provide job related training and practice for safe existence;

- Attitude towards safety and safe practices to be forged into the psyche;
- Quiet hours to contemplate on safety helps in introspection and understanding;
- cultivating a culture of safety.

Just like diseases and immunity of human body the accidents have roots in the human mind, and their preventives too exist in human mind! The key to safety is in the mind of man. It has been wisely said by Abraham Lincoln, "Next to creating a human life, the best thing a man can do is to save one".

Safety audit has been able to reinforce in the mind of the managers to 'own' operation as well as to 'own' the safe maintenance. Only operation without safe maintenance will be at the cost of human life and machines, only safe maintenance without operation is not at all economically viable. Therefore a balance is to be struck between the two.

Self-preservation is an inherent instinct in man. Everybody wants to preserve oneself, nobody wants to die for nothing. Then why accident? Men work for money no doubt but he takes risk of his life, even at the cost of his family just for praise, just for recognition. Same men jump into the unachieveable, they want to be adventures they want to be challenger. Nothing bad about it. But not in lieu of precious human life, not in lieu of morale of men.

Another psychological root of error is self concept. It is what a person thinks himself to be, not what others think about him. There is an inconsistency between what he thinks himself to be and what he actually is. This wrong conception often makes ones own assessment erroneous and the human being becomes a victim of his own misconception. Even after training inputs, regular attitudinal counselling individuals often indulge in unsafe and irrational acts due to this wrongful bloated self-concept about oneself which are normally not expected from such individuals. Line Managers and HRD Professionals are to be more observant on this psychological aspect also.

33

A Reflective Note on Accidents

Health of Machines and Men

A hypothesis is not a theory, it cannot be proved. Accident proneness is also a hypothesis about human behaviour which says, "accidents happen frequently to some men as a result of some behavioural characteristics unique to individual. In the context of mining activity, the accident proneness of a miner (he who works in the mine) can be not only due to the behavioural trait of the miner but also may be due to managerial lapses. Accidents are not by chance but are logical happenings of a combination of circumstances.

As per well-researched statistics, as the date changes one miner somewhere in the country dies in accident. Almost all mines accidents are attributed to:

- physical conditions (locational constraints);
- natural calamities (earthquake, fault movement, flood);
- systemic lapses (material failures, late communication);
- erroneous human acts (omissions and commissions).

Accident theorists have condensed the causes of accidents into two: unsafe acts and unsafe conditions; the unsafe conditions have in their core 'unsafe-acts' as their origin. An unsafe act therefore can cause irreparable loss like the loss of a human life. Any compensation against loss of human life is a token of gesture only and cannot be a substitute.

It is also observed sometimes that even minimum safety norms are not adhered to while rushing to meet production targets and aspiring for congratulations from superiors. Therefore reports are to be truthfully scrutinised as to whether it is inflatory (as regards availability of equipments, utilisation, production etc.) or inaccurate (as regards working conditions, work-ethics, adherence to safety norms etc.) R.N. Mishra Committee Report on the conduct and behaviour of coal mine manager is an eye-opener and is of academic interest. The fundamental problem with errant managers is not so much of their ignorance of weakness of the system but their refusal to know about them. Therefore miners in general (workers and managers) are to undergo to a revolution in attitude. Until things change managers would prefer to justify failures rather than ascertain reasons behind their occurrence for correction.

In our country professionalism is becoming a way of life because capacity utilisation of machines in the industries is not a common sight. Newer methods are being adopted in almost every branch of mining to maximise returns.

Like the routine health examination for working men health checkups for mining equipments are done through routine condition monitoring (RCM), a technique for machines, being used globally in order to minimise chances of unexpected machine break-downs. RCM is nothing but the technique of application of instrumentation and measurements to evaluate the conditions of a machine or any component as regards its ability to perform the desired functions. Persistent use of this technique over long periods improves equipment utilisation and escalates the economics of mining. Good health of machines is also necessary for the better life of the workforce.

OMS (output per man shift) has long been used as an indicator for efficiency. As long as investment is minimum OMS carries sense but in a highly mechanised mine where investment is very high OMS alone cannot be accepted as the efficiency indicator. In such cases the economics of production depends primarily on machine utilisation which is measured in terms of the duration of machine availability. A British study shows that by improving machine utilisation in coal-mining by only one per cent lead to wealth generation of 80 million pounds RCM over the years also indicated reduction of rate of accident.

Experienced managers of mining have indicated some parameters for RCM viz. Shock pulse of vibration (for health of bearing), Debris content in gear oil (for health of rares) etc. Even after taking corrective measures if there is no rectification then a fault is apprehended in the material.

However there is a critical value of machine utilisation for a particular mine beyond which the cost of production rises sharply and becomes uneconomical. Power failure, non-compatible support and machines, poor organisation, lack of spare availability, frequent breakdown of appliances, material failures due to poor quality and fabricational defect are detrimental to optimum machine utilisation.

Whenever the safety week is observed in the mines of different safety regions (under DGMS) it is said to be the time of gala enjoyment, pomp and show but the very essence of this observance is to introspect what we do and what we are supposed to do, it also gives opportunity for people involvement, to generate correct public understanding to think safe, to act safe and live safe, in larger interest organisation, society and government.

34

Role of Safety in Changing Economic Scenario

Industry and agriculture are the bones and flesh of a developing country like India. These two govern most of our economy. With the economic growth of our country, the priorities are changing to be more competitive, the competition transcends the local to the global, to be more quality oriented through refining the process for desirable results, etc.

Mining, the exploitation of mineral from mother earth has contributed in no small measure to the economic advancement of our country as a whole through domestic consumption and export. Mining activities are both capital and labour intensive. Mobility of traditional agricultural workers to mining industry, necessitates their exposure to skill, to avoid hidden job-hazards: lack of safety consciousness amongst such workers becomes less cost-effective in long run. The education of the entire staff must be continuous and dynamic, for the working conditions are constantly changing and solutions are constantly needed for the new problems which arise with regard to safety, health and environment: all these three have a symbiotic relationship. Therefore for achieving the task of multiple objectives of industrial planning with maximum focus on productivity, safety and optimal utilisation of resources available, we are to strive continuously for the broad objective of economic growth with social justice.

Development is not just about factories, dams, roads etc. Development is basically about the people. An industry with safe working and accident-free manpower is ideally what we call development.

Safety is the key component to achieve excellence, because it gives a psychological impetus that 'It is safe', 'I am safety working', 'Unless I work with care I may be prone to accident'.

Therefore in order to achieve psychosomatic freedom one has to:

- create constancy of purpose for improvement of products and services;
- acceptance of poor product and service is an obstacle to productivity;
- continually strive to find and fix the problem;
- drive out fear from organisation;
- encourage education and self-improvement for everybody.

Further more what India requires now is improved maintenance. Well-maintained and reliable equipment allows an operator to operate safely, to be consistent in output and quality. An unpredictable equipment will not only take its toll on human life but also add to cost. For this certain action points are suggested:

- Introduction of maintenance planners located in and focussing on the needs of each production department rather than through an impersonal system. Anticipation and prevention are the key jobs;
- Introduction on maintenance inspectors whose jobs are devoted to monitoring equipment performance and reporting back when action is indicated;
- Introduction of formalised and carefully structured unit training on basic maintenance skills.

There is a nexus between production and safety of human beings. Productivity is vital for the viability and growth of any industry and the economy of the country as a whole. The higher the productivity the higher is the growth and prosperity. Amongst all the resources human performance is the key to the success; because by optimising human performance alone one can optimise system performance. Any sort of accident preventive efficiency of the work-group. This impact on the morale is invisible and unquantifiable but has ill-effects. To some extent it severs the umbilical cord between the individual employee and the organisation. Once an accident occurs, there is trauma to the injured, whatever may be the corrective measures, the witness to the accident never remain the same person. Therefore, preventive safety measures yield better results, psychologically as well as from cost-effective point of view. In essence work situation is to be carefully planned for its safe execution. Safety, productivity and economy are inseparable and any disruption of this symbiotic relation damages the morale and economic fibre of any system which may be an industry, a state or a country.

There exists an enforcement body for safety as well as labour. Such a need arises because following safety practices and labour laws are considered by the industrialists as deterrent to profit and very often there are reported flouting the provisions. As a result safety is yet to become a way of life, and whatever is achieved otherwise is an apparent achievement where the fear of unsafety is hidden as a negative contribution. We are behind the most developed countries where accident-free operation is the motto. Human resource is viewed by them is very costly and they cannot afford any loss of life, whatsoever. Their mind-set is more capital intensive than labour whereas our mindset is just the contrary. Possibly for this reason our growth rate is very slow if the units of global order is used in expressing the gross output.

What is of crucial significance is to stay alert. The nine switches are:

- Sense of danger, interest of opportunity. A stimulating job triggers similar response;

- Muscular activity is also a stimulant for alertness but most of the jobs for which alertness is crucial is sedentary for the people. Where vigorous exercise is not possible a walk around helps;
- Pay attention to human biological clock. Remember that people feel drowsy in mid-afternoon and are most alert at mid-morning and late-afternoon. There is also a prime-time for individual human activity;
- Sleep-back balance. It depends since how long had one last sleep. A short nap also helps a lot;
- Stimulating drink or beverages are only short-lived and has a side-effect;
- Bright light makes a man alert. Light level has to be same as natural;
- Regulating temperature and humidity do help like a cold or warm shower;
- Sound has dual effect to make sleepy or alert. Use as per necessity;
- Environment aroma has also good effect. Light pepperment has a general appeal.

Finally, safety of men and machines has a crucial contribution towards the generation of economy at the grass-root level industrial activity. In a more liberalised and open, economic policy, like ours safety too, like other components, has an important role to play. It has both visible and invisible effects which has an indelible mark on the economy.

35

Employees Role in Balancing Safety, Health and Environment

Industry and agriculture, are the bones and flesh of a developing country like ours. Mining, the industrial exploitation of mineral from mother earth contributes in no small measures to the economy. Mobility of traditional agricultural workers to mining industry necessitates their exposure to skill, to avoid hidden job-hazards; because lack of safety consciousness amongst such workers becomes less cost-effective in the long run.

Industries are people-oriented so economic growth cannot be left to chance or luck but to people only. HRD approach or people-oriented approach helps people to increase self-control and responsibility while creating congenial environment in which each and everyone may contribute their mite to his maximum limit. Therefore more and more interactive sessions help people to understand the crucial role a man plays in the generation and growth of economy. An ancient proverb says, "Give a person a fish, and you feed that person for a day; teach a person how to fish and you feed that person for life".

Development is not just about factories, dams, roads etc. Development is basically about the people. An industry with accident-free health, manpower working in congenial atmosphere is ideally what we call development. Development should lead to progress and better quality of life. Progress of industrial activity is rapid and substantial in our country. It has also spread to regions with low levels of pollution, while it is concentrated is existing urban areas. It has adversely affected in terms of overcrowding by the unauthorised settlements, poor sanitation, shortage of potable water, housing and wastage disposal. All these affect the health of man and his habitat.

Amongst all the resources human performance is the key to success; because by optimising human performance alone one can optimise system performance. Therefore an employee's umbilical cord is linked with the health of the equipment and environment. By severing this cord there is either loss of human life or loss of equipment or damage to environment and all these affect adversely towards cost.

It is a long way ahead to go no doubt but giving a people-oriented approach to safety, health and environment and a judicious balance of these parameters directs growth both qualitatively and economically. The following are required to be instilled deep into the psyche of the people serving any industry:

- By the people only organisational safety and environment improves;
- Good health means good work and good thought;
- Human acts do cause accidents;
- Only to perform is rudimentary act but to act keeping in view one's own health, environment and safe-work is 'excellent performance'.

Above all human life is precious. Every human being is prone to accident. It is therefore ethical from existential point of view that each of us should not only protect ourselves from accidents but also ensure safer environment so that others do not fall victim to unsafety. This will transcend the industrial population to a more human and more productive level. Wasteful loss of human life and machines are shameful in a civilised world. It is therefore the responsibility of each of us to ensure good health, safe working conditions and congenial environment for ourselves only, through our own awareness that we can survive with the growth of industry otherwise we shall perish with the industry if we become more prone to accidents, pollute our own environment and are not healthy enough to contribute our brain and brown to the output.

With the ever-growing pace of industrialisation aided by fast-developing technology, employees are to carry the burden of progress. Efforts to identify accident repeaters or recidivists have indicated that they tend to be critical of authority, disorganised, careless, and impulsive with a strong concentration on immediate rather than long-term goals. Workman inspectors, participative, fora clarity in thoughts and actions of opinion leaders and practitioners etc. are of crucial significance. As working conditions are constantly changing and solutions are constantly needed for the new problems. These problems arise out of safety, health and environment and these three have a symbiotic relationship with employee at its fulcrum.

No theory or plan or govt. policy will make a business a success but it can only be done by the people. The mind-set of the people is required to be enriched by:

- Concept of masses pervaded every aspect of industry and society;
- Every thought we think is creating our future;
- Problems are only solutions in disguise;
- Do important jobs now before they become urgent;
- Trust the other as 96 per cent of them are trustworthy.

Since every action and activity howsoever infinitesimally small it may be does affect the totality in some form or other. Preventive measure by each and every employee while acting through thought, speech and work is advisable. The approach therefore should be one of preventive rather than after-the-fact correction, which is more often than not the case. Every employee, as such has a role to play to have a psychosomatic freedom through:

- Careful problem assessment;
- Continually strive to find and fix the problem;

- Introspection of dos and don'ts;
- Self-improvement through awareness and interest to know and accept changes which are beneficial;
- To share ideas and thoughts with others;
- Practising the science of ergonomics;
- Reporting and monitoring to be a way of life and part of in-built system.

Three major guiding principles are required for any Work-system.

1. ***Commitment of Employees***
   - Teamwork
   - Flexibility
   - Commitment to excellence
   - Continuous improvement
   - Innovation and creativity
2. ***Commitment of Company***
   - Common standard in treatment
   - Personal and professional growth
   - Competitive terms and conditions
   - Communication and involvement
   - Stable employment
3. ***Expectation of Employees***
   - Quality of life and living
   - Growth through working life

Employee is to be very clear of the following:

- My world of work
- My working relation
- My social relation

- What my colleagues expect from my working role
- What my family expects from my social role
- Preparedness to accept new structures
- Shift from disruption to suggestive approach
- Practice of personal skills, operating skills and maintenance skills as self-containing
- Facing more personal challenge and ability to accept change for the better
- Auditing one's own skill

Management process should be both democratic and dictatorial; democratic (participative approach) in 'decision making' but dictatorial (directive approach) in implementation. There are three basic levels where life is at danger:

(a) At life-input level like air, water, livestock, vegetation etc.

(b) At process level like producing industry, preparation of food-stuff, washing, revolving wheel etc.

(c) At consequential release level like effluents, gas leakage, garbage, waste etc.

At all these three levels permissible limits what we call 'safe limits' have been prescribed and any breach of these limits have often led to hazards and the human life falls a prey to this.

Say the case of air we know the ratio of oxygen, nitrogen and any increase in the pollutants like carbon monoxide, acetylene, benzene etc. there is danger to life. Similarly for water once the specifications to parts per million (ppm) has been defined if not adhered to becomes a potential threat to human life. Per litre of water if bacteria is more than 1 mg., fluoride more than 2.40 etc. water becomes a threat. Sound has its limit, more than 50 decibels may slowly lead to death (at 180 decibel). Vegetation, livestock are infested with pesticides, fertiliser chemicals but whether within limits is not known.

At process level, while preparing food we do not know that even after washing, boiling etc. even some chemicals withstand the high temperature to subsequently affect human body and mind. While cleaning with detergents, soaps etc. irritation at respiratory tracts, allergies have been reported.

Ultimately at the consequential release level we have industrial effluents injected into rivers, due to errors isocyanide gas leaks, radioactive waste disposal (if contains more than 0.3 roentgen may deteriorate human and animal health irreparably. Domestic sewerage, garbage disposal, varieties of industrial wastes are as important as industrial manufacturing. Unless timely disposal is done or such wastes are destroyed or recycled without any damage to the environment the product and garbage will form a vicious circle.

Some pollutants are biodegradable which are to be treated through; primary (mechanical screening, sedimenting, burning, burying etc.), secondary (biological reduction of organic matter, through natural or micro-organism decomposition), and tertiary means (chemical removal of phosphates, nitrates, obstinate organics etc.). If the cost is 1 for primary it will be 5 and 10 for secondary and tertiary respectively.

There are nondegradable pollutants like discarded aluminium containers, metal foils, strong detergents, plastics, poly bags and hundreds of man-made discards which degrade very slowly and often end up as landfills.

The third kind of pollutants are poisons like salts of metals (mercury, lead etc.), smog gases, radioactive substances, pesticides and other toxicity whose impact on human life is not known completely.

Since pollutants are created by man, these can be destroyed by man only. Biodegradable and nondegradables are to be separated by man, the former to be used as fertilisers and latter recycled economically. Management of life is in the hands of man only.

Bionomics is the key word of today. It is the management of a house where man and nature cohabitate. Man while discharging any business function is required not only to look into the internal affairs of the business but also to its external impacts (good or bad). To survive as a living organism man is to give life support to his external environment. The role of the present man is that of a 'knowledge worker' which is based on social values. To consume resource, to consume energy are the currencies of today. Ecological values and economic values can be joined through adopting energy units instead of monetary units.

Therefore every employee is to contemplate on the various vitals like:

- Owning responsibility for choosing
- Using self-talk for effective thinking
- Choosing one's own personal rules for private and worklife
- Identifying the right perception of things that matter
- Predicting and creating one's own future
- To exercise mind's eye for total perception
- Learning to understand other's stand, to work with other
- Identify and own perceptual and conceptual errors
- Predicting risk and reward
- Not to misattribute to the cause of problems
- Contemplating on what environment does to us
- Learning from observation not from heresay.

36

Solving Safety Issues Through Participative Management

Changing Profiles Management and Workforce

For several years since industrialisation, industrial engineering believed that productivity will improve if and only if the average skilled worker is glued to his machines all the eight hours, strictly following the repetitive operational steps, totally unmindful of colleagues, lunch, tea breaks, noise, even calls of nature. Personnel and IR specialists ensured that clocking the entry and exit of workers is linked to disciplinary measures. Technical training specialists try to equip technical skills which make the worker more equipment friendly and observe safe work practices.

In short, for a long time worker was not perceived as a human capable of relating, creating and contributing, using his own initiative and motivation to utilise his freedom to perform meaningful acts for the organisation. But today the profiles of management and workforce are changing:

- Management, in addition to production and productivity are concerned about safety, environment and health. They have changed their mind-set to productivity, performance and participation (3 Ps for progress).

- Workforce has transcended the status of mere wage-earners. There is abundance of intelligent and knowledge workers who are sensitive, responsive and responsible.

These changing profiles have implications for the management and unions:

(a) Implications for Management

- workers understand planning, strategy and market share-value;
- knowledge workers understand at ground level and know loopholes of top-level planning;
- supervisory cadre will vanish and better job content will be required;
- self-manager sections by workers shall mushroom;
- planned career path will be expected;
- more domocratic, less authoritarian behaviour will be expected;
- unnecessary expenditure will be severely questioned.

(b) Implications for Unions

- new generation workers will not join strikes nor any kind of mass action;
- workers will expect unions to demand for improvement in quality of work-life and social life;
- genuinely democratic and developmental unicn will be liked;
- more driven by issues than ideologies.

Employer-Employee Participation

Democratisation of industry can only be through participation. Participation means vertical involvement, delimiting hierarchical boundaries. Collation, storage and dissemination of information is done through participation to make the participating partners more 'responsive' and 'responsible'.

Participation between the employee and the employer yields fruits of immense values viz.

- Helps involvement and joint decision making
- Builds team-work
- Increases personal challenge and confidence, better self-management
- Enables individuals to reach their full potential
- Fosters harmony
- Eliminates demarcation
- Stops the feeling of exploitation
- Helps in sharing information and consultation

The following table is a comprehensive representation of participation in industrial context:

Level of Participation	Areas of Participation	Coverage of Participation
Shop-floor/section	Technological	Production, procedure, tools, norms of productivity etc.
Department/division	Social	Grievance, health, safety, township, welfare, sanitation
Organisational	Economic	Profit-loss, cost control, efficiency, market strategy
Corporate	Political	Govt. parties, customers, suppliers

Through information sharing and consultation there occurs attitudinal change and when there is joint decision making and self-management the attitudinal change grows to organisational change.

Responsibility lies with the employer and the employees to make participation a success. Pre-requisites for participating management are:

- to believe in participation;
- respect for individual and his statement;
- to ensure just dealings;

- to hear patiently criticisms and pitfalls;
- open mind to learn;
- to imposition;
- to be on the same platform and wavelength of discussion;
- gradual movement

Similarly pre-requisites for participating employees are:

- responsible behaviour;
- use of less emotion and more logic;
- organisational loyalty;
- no criticism or vigilant observation;
- to be open to avail training and education for better participation

To participative forums are policy making bodies, therefore the participants shall have a scientific approach and dynamic attitude of mind to make the work place safe and healthy to work.

Safety—A Thrust Area

Safety is "freedom from unacceptable risk of harm". And risk has following connotation:

- *Risk:* A combination of profitability of occurrence of harm and the severity of that harm.
- *Tolerable Risk:* Risk which is accepted in a given context based on the current values of society.
- *Residual Risk:* Risk remaining after protective measures have been taken.
- *Risk Analysis:* Use of available information to identify hazardous events and to estimate the risk.

Thrust on safety awareness is a joint responsibility of the employer and the employees. Communication forums should be developed. Trade unions and management have a symbiotic role to play jointly. SWOT analysis of the issue of safety reveal the following:

Strengths

Concerned work force at skilled level;

Automation and computerisation;

Proactive managerial decision making.

Weaknesses

Semi-literacy among unskilled work force;

Drinking habits among tribals;

Old mind-set.

Opportunities

Audio-visual media;

Preventive maintenance.

Threats

Obsolescence of machines and/or methods;

Unsafe practices;

Competition in market.

Safety is a thrust area due to its unpredictability. Since there is accident there is loss of human life, which is costly. The causes of safety issues can be either due to man and/or due to machine. These issues are to be identified by the participative forums. Each of the issue its cause and possible solution to be discussed threadbare by the participating members without any prejudice and criticism. Job content and finite element analysis of each job/activity to be made risk-free.

Tripartite forum exists for safety. But at bipartite level no compromise can happen in regard to safety measures, some of the issues can be reviewed by the participative forum:

- Is the planning and design for elimination hazard adequate?
- Are the statutory provision followed?
- Whether there is 100 per cent employee participation and understanding of safety?

- Is safety treated as of same value as operation and production?
- Is education, training, retraining and publicity on safety sufficient?
- What does the annual check up reveals?
- Is there continuous monitoring of safety plans and activities?
- Is there conscious effort for better living condition within workplace and outside?
- Have all potential hazards been identified and rectified?
- Are disciplinary measures taken against who violate safety measures?
- Are suitable rewards given for effective observance?

Total Safety Management (TSM) is considered as an Integrated Organisational Approach for continuously monitoring and improving the safe system for prevention of accidents and dangerous occurrence so as to have zero loss of human life and organisation's property. This can be achieved only through co-operative participation of employer and employee. There is no question of blaming one another. All issues of safety can be solved if there is:

- commitment towards total safety;
- improvement of process activity;
- adoption of modern information system and analysis;
- statistical analysis of pattern and process control;
- determination of trend of accidents;
- identification of repetitive occurrence, if any and places/ people thereof;
- identification of causes (humans, machines or both);
- accountable system (executive deployment of safety officials);

- hazard warning system (use of sensors at work-sites/ hazardous spots);
- watchdog system (departmental scrutiny and surprise checking).

The factors which need to be relooked, have arisen out of changes in the organisation variables of work technology, people and environment. These must be analysed by the participating forums:

- job complexity;
- age-mix versus workload;
- self image matching the job content;
- degree of stress at work-site;
- stress indicators;
- simple and understandable outcome of participation forums;
- low accident organisation (LAO) and high accident organisation (HAO) have less and more absenteeism;
- absenteeism versus accident, statistical analysis.

The employer and employee participative forums must make others believe that:

- hazards can be made zero by safe performance of people;
- only people can improve safety in organisations;
- main causes of accidents are not only unsafe condition but also unsafe acts;
- to improve safety the attitude, moral awareness of people to be improved;
- task, work enrichment shall promote safety;
- bottom to top communication is very vital for safety promotion;
- employees are basically interested to work.

The issue of safety can be handled simultaneously from 'proactive' and 'reactive' angles. Its meaning is 'preventive' and 'corrective' respectively. So that life (people) stands victorious against death (disaster).

We have to synergise ourselves, both the employer and the employees together, to create and implement solutions for the strategic thrust areas in general and safety as a thrust area in particular, so that the pace of change is accelerated to maximise profit without any loss of life and property.

37

Practical Words

Word

One kind word has much more value, than it is believed. It motivates beyond imagination. Your own words make you what you are. Words can be egoless. You are the maker of words, make them palatable.

Responsibility

Pick up those who can accept responsibility. Try to match person with taste. The person performing may not do as good as you do but still go on building persons by giving low risk projects.

Meeting

Meetings are often used for firing and to demonstrate that the might is right. Instead meetings may be called at suitable time when participants are at their best. It should end at natural time like lunch break, closing office hour. Surprising meetings are of bad taste. Nobody likes. Nothing comes out of it.

Deadline

It is to be just in time. But meeting the deadline before it expires is a refreshing act of experience. Those who attain only they realise. Check before the deadline arrives mercilessly. Give due date for assignment and explain how this relates to other priorities and segments of work. Deadlines are to be met by you first, then others shall follow.

Way-out

Think...there must be a better way. What 'should be done' is more important than what 'one likes to do'.

Balance

The less you speak the more you will be heard. The more you speak the less you will be heard. Look around, look within and balance yourself. Head and heart when balanced shall yield action beyond question and doubt.

Wisdom

It is wise to do what you say, it is not always wise to say what you do. Are you wise or a fool? Wise man learn from others' mistakes, fools learn only from their own mistakes.

Unhappiness

It is best defined as the difference between our talents and our expectations. Understanding oneself gives happiness and peace.

Change

You must change with time unless you are influential enough to change the time. If you are not influential enough to change the time, you must change with time. Change yourself if you wish to change the world.

38

Expressions for Self-Realisation

- What you 'want to be' is more important that 'what you are'. It is easy to think but difficult to achieve.
- Attitude (not aptitude) determines your altitude.
- It is not enough to be good. Be good for something. Be good to somebody.
- Waste no more time discussing and arguing as to what a good man should be. Be one.
- Do great things without promising great things.
- If you try to please everybody, nobody will like you.
- Live in a manner that doesn't hurt anyone but leaves a mark on others.
- I am the people, the mob, the crowd, the team, the man. The work of the world is done through me.
- One man with courage makes a majority.
- Be focused in approach.
- Self knowledge is the beginning and knowing oneself is the end. Self correction makes a man successful.
- There can be no rainbow without a cloud or a storm.

- Let yesterday be lesson, today action, tomorrow hope.
- Don't believe in your fate, believe in your strength.
- Sensing, suffering and studying are pillars of learning.
- Anyone who is not confused doesn't really understand the situation.
- Action may not always bring happiness, but there is no happiness without action.
- Men of action shouldn't be diplomats. Because when a diplomat says 'yes' it means 'may be'. When he says 'may be' it means 'no'. When he says 'no' he is not a diplomat but a man of action.
- Obstacles are not stopping stones but stepping stones to climb over.
- Just by worrying things don't get better. Try to undo worry.
- It is always good to know many things but it is better to make use of whatever little we understand.
- The journey of life follows an unknown path.
- Both earth and heaven are within you. You know the earth but not the heaven within you.

39

Self Improvement Words

- *Strive for Excellence:* Being excellent is different from being good. Just being good is not enough. Excellence is an ever moving target and one has to constantly raise it for oneself.
- *Never Feel Inferior:* Remember no one can make you feel inferior without your consent. You have so many uniqueness. Just because someone is different from you doesn't mean that you are inferior.
- *Take Care of Yourself:* You need a lot of energy to deal with challenges. Unless you take care of your physical and mental well being there is no way you can take care of others.
- *Success is not Yours:* No success is individuals' achievement. It is the resultant of so many factors. Such thinking will preserve sense of humility and modesty, otherwise the feeling of success will make you vulnerable to make bad judgements.
- *Do not Worry:* It is natural that things don't go as expected. Why worry about things which are beyond your control. Remember yours is not always the best way. Trust that storms never last long.
- *You Are What You Are:* Everyone may not like you. Many will praise, few will criticise. You need no ones approval to be you. Your critics will give you a chance to re-look at yourself.

- *Grow Interest:* Never think that you have to stay where you are in life. Life is a flux, everybody it gives you opportunities to change. Accept change. Enjoy your own growth and live a life which is intense and meaningful.

40

Words in Work

Freedom

The ultimate aim of management is to give freedom to work.

Happiness

Enjoy life at every given point or moment. Any one enjoying life completely can handle any regrets.

Delegation

It is not giving power in absentia. It is the just the opposite of it.

Word

Unkind word cuts. Kind word heals.

Courage

Facing the results of your thinking and action is courage.

Suggestion

A strong suggestion may not influence immediately but fructifies at appropriate moment.

Thinking

- As you think so you become
- Persistence thinkers are few
- Clear thinkers are only a few
- Deep thinkers are very few.

41

Frequently Referred Management Words

Ab initio	From the beginning.
Accountability	Responsibility for results.
Ad hoc	For particular case in hand without considering wider effects.
Ad interim	For the intervening time/period.
Adjourn	To stop meeting or court for a period.
Adjudicate	To give judgement between two parties. (Low)
Administer	To manage especially in a setting that emphasises the application of fixed procedures and minimal environmental turbulence.
Administrator	Person who administers.
Adverse	Unfavourable.
Agent	Person who acts for, or who manages the business affairs of another or others.
Ageism	Unfair discrimination against older people.
Allocate	To divide resources among competing interests (allocating financial resources through a budgetary process is a prime example of such division).
Allocation	A quantity of resource allocated for a particular item.
Allowance	Money which is given for a special reason.

Amalgamation	Joining together of two or more groups/trade unions.
Amend	To change and make more correct or acceptable.
Amendment	Change to a document.
Andragogy	Science of adult-learning.
Annul	To cancel or to stop something being legal. The contract was annulled by the court.
Antedate	To put an earlier date on a document. The contract was antedated to January 1st.
Apply	To ask for something usually in writing. To implement/exercise.
A posteriori	From consequence (effect) to antecedent (cause).
Appraise	To assess the value of a property, a person's job performance or other items of value.
Approve	To think something is good. To agree to something officially.
Approximate	Not exact, but almost correct.
A priori	From antecedent (cause) to consequence (effect).
A propos	With reference to.
Aptitude	Ability (to do a task).
Arbitrate	To be chosen by both parties to try to settle industrial disputes.
Arbitration	Settling of disputes by special official outside the purview of a court of law.
Arbitration tribunal	Court which decided industrial disputes.
Argue	Discuss without agreeing.
Assert	To show that you have control or can make decisions.
Assets	The items of value owned by a Company or person.
Assume	To take for oneself. He has assumed responsibility of the post.
Attrition	Loss of labour through natural wastage.
Authority	The right to use assigned resources within one's discretion to accomplish an assigned task. It also includes the right to direct people and other resources. Power to do something.

Authorise	Give permission or power to do something.
Automation	Use of machines to work with very little supervision of people.
Autonomy	The ability to operate independent of other units.
Autonomous	Which rules itself.
Avert	To stop something happening. Averting a strike etc.
Benchmark	Point or level which is important and can be used as a reference when making evaluation or assessment.
Bias	Favouring one group or person rather than another.
Bilateral	Between two parties or countries.
Bona fide	Trustworthy or which can be trusted. With good faith implying the absence of fraud.
Boss	The person in charge or holding the final authority.
Brainstorming	Meeting to thrash out problems where everyone puts forward different ideas.
Breach	Failure to carry out the terms of a contract.
Budget	Process of allocating financial resources.
Bureau	(means 'desk' in French) Office which specialises.
Bureaucracy	System of administration where individual person's responsibilities and powers are strictly defined and processes are strictly followed.
Capacity	The maximum amount of product or service that could be provided by a given mechanism.
Capital	Wealth that an organisation possess to employ in achieving its aims.
Centre (or Center in US)	Establishment or complex where main activities occur.
CEO	Chief Executive Officer.
Certificate	Official document carrying an official declaration by someone and signed by him.
Certify	To make an official declaration in writing.
Change agent	Person or unit who induce change, diagnose problems, resolve conflicts etc.
Cliche	means stereotyped phrase (pronounced klee-shay).
Code of ethics	Guidelines or correct behaviour drawn up by a group/association for its members.

Code of practice	Rules drawn up by association/group which members must follow when doing business.
Collective	A group as a whole.
Committee	A group of people assigned to perform a given task as a group.
Communication	Transfer of meaning from one (the sender) to another (the receiver).
Conciliation	Bringing together the parties in dispute so that disputes can be settled.
Conduct	Way of behaving. To carry on to conduct meetings etc.
Confer	To discuss an issue/problem with another person or a group.
Conflict	Disagreement or clash in feelings and/or interests.
Conglomerate	A company made up of many other companies.
Conspiracy	Described the intention to break the law.
Constituencies	The various interest groups who vie for the attention of the organisation.
Control	The management function that aims to keep activities directed in such a way that desired results are achieved. Monitoring of performance.
Convene	To ask people to come together.
Convener	He who convenes.
Co-operation	Joint effort to achieve a desired result.
Co-ordinate	To integrate one's own efforts with those of others to achieve a desired result.
Counsel	To give professional advice to others on personal matters.
Coute que coute	(pronounced 'koot-ke-'koot') At all costs.
Credentials	Letters or documents which describe a person's qualities and skills.
Culpa lata	Gross negligence.
Culpa-levis	Slight negligence.
Decision	A determination. Settlement of a question. A course of actions consciously chosen from available alternatives for the purposes of achieving a desired result. Therefore, decision involves choice, conscious mental process and purpose.

Decruiting	Policy of replacing older people with younger ones.
De facto	Opposed to de jure, e.g. Uncle is a de facto guardian.
De jure	By right, as opposed to de facto, e.g. Father is a de jure guardian.
Domicile	Place where someone lives. He is domiciled in Madhya Pradesh.
Downgrade	To reduce the importance of someone or of a job.
Echelon	Group of people of certain grade in organisation. Communication has improved between higher and lower echelons of the Company.
Embezzle	To steal money which is not yours and which you are only looking after.
Entice	To persuade someone to do something. He enticed his neighbours servant by offering higher remuneration.
Ergonomics	Study of people at work and their working conditions.
Erode	To wear away gradually.
Estimate	Quantity assigned by approximate judgements.
En masse	(pronounced 'awn-massy') In mass.
En route	(pronounced 'awn-root') On the way.
Environment	Aspects, conditions or objects surrounding an organisation.
Empathy	Attempt to project oneself into the view point of the other.
Examine	To look at someone or something very carefully to see if it can be accepted.
Ex cathedra	From the chair. With official authority.
Exempli gratia (abbreviated as e.g.)	For the purpose of example.
Ex gratia	As a matter of favour or grace.
Ex offico	By virtue of an office.
Ex parte	Proceeding in absence of the other party by a court tribunal/enquiry.
Ex post facto	Made after the occurrence.
Experientia docet	Experience teaches.

Facsimile	(make it alike) an exact copy.
Faux pas	Mistake
Feme covert	A married woman.
Fame sole	An unmarried woman.
Forfeit	Lose as penalty. Thing or benefit lost by crime or fault.
Forge	To shape forcefully. To invent. Advance slowly and steadily.
Forgery	Tampered document, the act of doing it.
Forgo	To go without, to give up.
Formidable	Likely to be difficult.
Fons et origo (Latin)	The source and origin.
Forecast	Predict. Conjectural estimate of something to occur in future.
Forum	A court. Public Place for meeting/discussion.
Goals	The basic aims of an enterprise/organisation/group.
Grapevine	Unofficial communications network in an organisation. I heard that on the grapevine that Mr. X has been sacked.
Human Resource Management (HRM)	Responsibility for an organisation's productive use of and constructive dealings with its employees.
Ibidem, ibid, id	In the same place, volume or case.
Industrial Relations (IR)	An approach to management promoted by some behavioural scientists. The central theme is the relief or prevention of dissatisfaction among employees.
In camera	In secret session.
In cognito	In disguise.
In flagrante delicto (Latin)	In the act of doing something. The clerk was caught in flagrante delicto pocketing the petty cash.
Injunction	Court order telling someone not to do something.
In situ	In its own place, in its original position.
In status quo	In the position in which one was before.
Inter alia	Among other things.
Inter se	Among themselves.

In toto	Entirely, wholly.
Ipso facto	By the very nature of the case.
Ispo jure	By the law itself.
Interface	Area common to two or more systems/processes.
Job	Piece of work either to be done or completed.
Job description	An exposition of the duties and responsibilities that are inherent in a particular job.
Job enlargement	Includes more tasks or more kinds of tasks in a given job in order to make the job more satisfying.
Job enrichment	Changing some aspects of a job in order to satisfy more of a person's higher order needs.
Key	Important. Key personnel, key post, key staff etc.
Kickback	Illegal commission paid to someone (especially a govt. official) who helps in business deal.
Know-how	Skill or ability in a particular field.
Labour unions	Organisations of workers banded together to promote workers' interests, especially higher wages and better fringe benefits and working conditions.
Liaise	To inform someone of what is being done, so that actions are co-ordinated.
Liaison	Keeping someone informed as to what is happening.
Line management job	A managerial job that includes supervision and one of the central business function such as production or selling. It is frequently contrasted with staff jobs.
Liquidate	To terminate an operation by disposing of all the assets, returning the proceeds to the owners of operation.
Logistics	The function of moving, storing and distributing resources and goods.
Mala fide	Bad faith. Opposite to good faith.
Manage	To mobilise resources for the achievement of human purpose.
Management	The group of persons who manage the organisation; also the discipline concerned with the understanding and improving the knowledge of how to manage.
Management Development	The means by which the organisation contributes to the development of the managerial abilities of its management group.

Management science	An approach that emphasises the application of scientific methods for the improved understanding and practice of management.
Management Information System (MIS)	The term describes a management's mechanism for obtaining, processing, storing, retrieving and using information frequently suggesting use of computers. An all inclusive system for providing management with information for efficient decision making.
MBO	Management by objective. A systematised idea for setting clear and definite objective for each individual at all hierarchical levels, usually through joint participation of superior and subordinate.
Memorandum (or 'Memo' in short)	Short message sent from one person to another.
Merit	Quality which deserves reward.
Meritocracy	Society or organisation where advancement is based on a person's natural ability rather than his or her background.
Militant	Person who actively supports and works for a cause.
Mission	Tasks to be performed. An organisation's paramount objective for its immediate future.
Motivation	Personal mechanism that moves an individual to action.
OB	Organisation Behaviour. The study of the behaviour of individuals in organisation from the angle of behavioural sciences.
OD	Organisation Development. A planned organisation wide effort for participating in continuous rethinking and changing beliefs, values and structures to adapt to new challenges.
OR	Operational Research. A scientific as well as qualitative approach where a team of diverse specialists contribute in order to seek an optimum solution. The discipline that studies the application of mathematical tools and logic to the solution of industrial problems.
Ombudsman	Official who investigates complains by the public against govt. departments. Management employee who is given the freedom to move around the work place to locate and remedy unfair practices.

Optimisation	The process of finding the best possible solution to a management problem usually using an operation Research model.
Organisation Chart	A pictorial representation of the formal organisation.
Organising	The process of breaking a task to be performed into subtasks and creating a formal organisational structure.
Ostracism	Rejection of a member from a group by other members.
Participative management	An approach to improving management practice that emphasises participation of all impacted parties in decisions.
Per se	By itself.
Per pro	(per procurationem) with the authority of the secretary signed per pro the manager.
Performance	Denotes the achievements of positive results. Actual results obtained.
Personnel appraisal	The evolution of employees performance and interaction between a boss and subordinate.
Personnel Management	The management of firm's human resources.
PERT Chart	(Programme, Evaluation, Review Technique) It is a planning technique that uses charts created by the Navy to aid in planning a project and evaluating its progress after it is under way.
Planned obsolescence	An approach to design that utilises the expectation that the existing design will become out of vogue.
Planning	The management function that includes decisions and actions to insure future results.
Policy	A specified mode of approaching a particular area in future.
Post mortem	After death: Surgical examination of a dead body to find the cause of death.
Power	Ability to influence, to make others act in a way desired by the holder of power.
Procedures	Specified ways to approach narrowly defined situations.

Pro rata	in proportion.
Pro tem	for the time being.
Productivity	The production per production employee.
Prototype	A model of a potential new product used to evaluate product prospect.
Quasi	In some sense or aspect but not in every sense.
Quid pro quo	(Something for something) consideration.
Quorum	Minimum prescribed number to be competent for transaction.
Ratify	To approve officially by the apex body. The proposal is to be ratified by the Board next week.
Reductio ad absurdum	The method of improving an argument by showing that it leads to an absurd conclusion.
Reprimand	Official criticism to an employee. After receiving a reprimand he knew he would be sacked.
Repudiate	To refuge to accept.
Retrospective	Effective from past date.
Res nullius	A thing which has no owner.
Resume	Summary (pronounced rezum-ay).
Satisficing	An attempt to find a satisfactory solution which need to be exact optimum. Word coined by H.A. Simon to contrast with optimising.
Sang froid	Coolness under agitating circumstances.
Scab	Worker who goes on working when there is strike.
Scientific management	An approach to management advocated by Frederick W. Taylor. Its core is the organised study of work, the analysis of work into its simplest elements and the systematic improvements of workers' performance of each of these elements resulting high level of output per worker.
Sic	Found within brackets after a word or expression in a quoted passage. It indicates that the quotation is exact.
Sinecure	Job which is well-paid but involves very little work.
Sino anno	Without date.
Sine die	Adjournment to a date but not at the moment.
Sphinx	Enigmatic man who keeps his thought and plan secret.

Simulation	An abstract replication of certain of the dynamics of a problem situation.
Social impact	The final consequences of actions that go beyond the consequences that are action's raison d'etre.
Staff	Individual contributors who advise or counsel rather than directly manage a group of people, in contrast to line managers.
Strategy	Plan to achieve task. An organisation's basic approach in achieving its overall objectives.
Structure	Framework of an organisation.
Status quo	That state in which things were.
Suggestio falsi	A false suggestion.
Supressio Veri	Wilful concealment of truth.
System	A set of inter related parts.
Systems approach	Viewing a subject as a whole composed of inter dependent parts and delineated by clear boundaries.
System thinking	Analysis that uses systems and their dynamics to examine problems and possible solutions.
Tactics	Basic approaches to be used in carrying out a predetermined strategy.
Task force	A group assigned to accomplish a task.
Team	A group of people who are expected to work together on a project.
Technology	A way or means to accomplish a task. The technology may or may not use machines.
Time management	Allocation of one's time assigning priorities, identifying, eliminating time wasters for efficiently reaching the goals.
Ultra vires	Implies beyond power or capacity. It may or may not be illegal. A rule is ultra vires when it is beyond the rule-making power.
Union	An organisation that brings the workmen in a trade or industry together for the purpose of bargaining collectively for improved wage, benefit and working conditions.
Utility	The usefulness or inherent value of something as perceived by an individual or an organisation.

Vet	To examine very carefully.
Via media	Middle way. Through a middle man.
Vice versa	The order being reversed.
Vis-a-vis	The relationship of one of two persons (or things) to the other, when facing (or situated) opposite to each other.
Viva Voce	Oral testimony.
Wealth	The sum total of economic valuables owned by an individual, a country or a society.
Yardstick	Means of measuring results in key areas of business.
Zero-based budgeting	Budgeting which assumes that each project or activity must justify again any expenditure (above zero) for each new year even if the project activity was justified previously.

42

Management Aphorisms

Depression	–	It is corrosive, don't allow it. As such it doesn't stay, it goes. Expedite its departure intentionally otherwise it corrodes deep within.
Rainbow Recognition	–	Chief Executive Officers must be able to connect with a wide spectrum of talented people.
Departure	–	Don't hang on too long. Depart at desirable time; don't overstay. Departure is more important than arrival.
Top Mistake	–	Top man's mistake is very costly and sometimes fatal too.
Mouth	–	In man the gateway to soul; in woman, the outlet of the heart.
Vision	–	Many don't have any vision. However they are not blind at all in their day to day activity. A visionary exists in future with his foot on earth; once he is footloose he balloons up, up into the sky!
Wealth	–	We do not create wealth by manufacturing material objects, but by satisfying people's wants, and needs...
Eccentric	–	"We might define an eccentric as a man who is a low unto himself; and a crank too who, having determined what the law is, insist on laying it down on others".

Shortcuts	–	One pays heavy price for taking short cuts for solving problems.
Predictability	–	Rules and laws help make behaviour predictable. Total reliance on rules and directives is not a good way to assure success.
Success	–	Success attracts criticism. Learn to handle it with maturity.
Future	–	Sex, violence and tantalising visuals are fast becoming an integral part of our children's lives our generation's future resources! The future need not be only an extrapolation of the past.
Art and Science	–	Appreciate art, not just science. And do not miss the wood for the trees.
Failure	–	Persistence pays. And in every failure there is a lesson. Absorb it.
Human Management	–	A smile on one's lips and a pat on the back means the same in any language...The first lesson in the human side of management (Thomas Teal in Harvard Business Review Dec' 96).
Success	–	The more successful one becomes, the more vulnerable he feels. Success is also a lousy teacher. It seduces smart people into thinking they can't lose! (Bill Gates in The Road Ahead) Success is defined as flattening the competition, not creating excellence.
Sex	–	No one sex can govern alone. I believe that one of the reasons why civilisation has failed so lamentably is that it has had one-sided government. (Nancy Astor "My Two Countries).
Source	–	At least know the source of your inspiration. You may need it to extend the campaign later.
Pragmatism	–	What is important is not what is right or wrong but what works or doesn't.
Totalitarian	–	L'etat, c'est moi (The state, it is I) Louise XIV, King of France (1638-1715).
Economy	–	Economy, which in things inanimate is nothing but money making; but when exercised over men becomes policy. Plutarch (Lives Crasus).

Production – We have no more right to consume happiness without producing it than to consume wealth without producing it. (George Bernard Shaw, Candida).

People – People are most valuable assets and have the immense capability of achievements.

Leader – Only one man in a thousand is a leader of men—the other 999 follow women. (Groucho Marx).

Injury – The manager who spares the bad in fact injures the good.

Today and Tomorrow – What you can do today don't wait for tomorrow, do it today itself but if you can do it tomorrow as well in a better way yielding good dividends for larger cause than never do today. Do tomorrow.

Belief – Don't be misled into believing that somehow the world owes you a living. He who believes that his parents, govt. or anyone else owes him a livelihood and that he can collect it without labour shall one day wake up to discover himself working for another fellow who did not have that belief and therefore earned the right to have others work for him. (David Sarnoff).

Registration – Galbraiths law states that anyone who says he won't resign four times, will. (John Kenneth Galbraith).

Deliberation vs Action – Deliberation is the work of many men; Action of one alone. (Charles de Gaulle).

Doubt – The trouble is the stupid are sure of themselves what they say, what they do but the intelligent are full of doubt.

Image – In every key office there is at least one man whose primary goal is polishing its image.

Understanding – Understanding must precede decision. Otherwise consequence is disastrous and often irreparable. A hanged man can't be made alive.

Orphan – Learn to shoulder an orphan as because success has many fathers but failure is an orphan. None claim an orphan.

Mind Set – A beginning is not made for the feeling that the objectivity cannot be achieved in its entirety. This mindset is precisely the greatest obstacle to progress.

Causes – The causes of events are ever more revealing than the events themselves. (–Cicero).

Destiny – Confused folks sometimes cannot understand bad management and curse destiny. But not always.

Imagination – Imagination is creativity and it is more important than knowledge itself. It defines freedom of thought and action.

Death – Don't be overawed by death.

Routine – Remember that disruption of normal managerial activities in abnormal times demoralise the workers, the public.

Pointless delegation – Delegation without constant verification is pointless. Delegation without control is sterile. Always cross-check and verify.

Intolerance – Nothing bad about intolerance of carelessness and mistakes. Be intolerant. Be firm.

Mistakes – Mistakes do not matter. A person who doesn't make mistakes makes nothing else.

Youngs – Encourages young minds, work with young minds grow with young minds. Otherwise how can you teach boys of your age and younger than you?

Rocks and Monuments – Today's rocks can be tomorrow's monuments.

Good and Bad – Don't say all is bad. Ask what you have done to make it good.

Competitors – Train your competitors. They will thank you, they will respect you and through competition even improve your skills!

Failure – Failure after implementation is pardonable but failure without effort is detestable.

Memory – Keeping in memory and using is bad; memories may fail but minutes never do. So in a meeting never keep proceedings in mind, draw a minute.

Questions – Don't be overawed and silent. Study papers in meeting. Ask questions if you have to. If you don't do this you will find yourself in a mess.

Key players – Appoint key players to a management team is like moving chess pieces: one blunder can cost you the entire game.

Interview	–	An old saying has it that "every man complains of his judgement". This is so very true for an interview situation where the sophisticated executives tend to overrate vastly their ability to interrogate a candidate. Only one interview to evaluate the subtleties of human behaviour is not sufficient—this is the fallacy of interviewer insight.
Success	–	"Successful People go on being successful". This is the essence of Peter Principle which says that managers inevitably rise to their levels of competence. Those who rise to position are usually promoted based on their past successes, which are often irrelevant to future promotion! What is over looked is that the prior successes has already brought the candidate to his incompetence threshold; continuing success is therefore fallacious.
Industrial Revolution	–	The industrial revolution was probably the most important event in world history; since the invention of the agriculture and cities. (Eric Hobsbawm: "The Age of Revolution).
Insight	–	Group interviewes, group discussions are like "beauty contests" which goes favourably for extroverted candidates. Attention is diverted from the indices of 'personality weakness'. Group insight is fallacious.
Reference checking	–	Bloated references of self are often given by candidates. Past employers do not prefer to give adverse information. 'Family background' and 'as-is where-is objective analysis' of individual is important and of crucial significance.
Scientific testing	–	Psychological or behavioural testing through structured proforma is only an art not a science. Sometimes test takers fake answers. Rorschach Inkblot (RI) or Wareham Mc Murry Incomplete Sentence Blanck (WMISB) can be revealing provided it is administered properly and analysed by a qualified skilled practitioner.
Whole-person	–	More information is collected, more accurate is the evaluation. It is true for man. Key pieces of the puzzle shouldn't be missing. Measure values, work habits, judgement, maturity, ability to function under pressure, people skills and leadership are equally important as other aspects for whole-person evaluation.

Trivials – What seems trivial and routine today becomes history tomorrow. It is to be recorded howsoever trivial it may seem to be; it will show up later as a mistake to learn from an achievement to better on.

Economics – The economist, like every one else, must concern himself with the ultimate aims of life. (Alfred Marshall in Principles of Economics).

Corrupt influence – Corrupt influence which is itself the perennial spring of all prodigality, and of all disorder, which loads us, more than million of debt; which takes away vigour from our arms wisdom from our councils, and every shadow of authority and credit from the most vulnerable parts of our constitution. (Edmond Burke).

Words – At the end of the day you are the words you have read, spoken and the words you have written and perhaps a little more. (Robert Musil "Precision of the Soul").

Wealth – Wealth is not without its advantages... But beyond doubt, wealth is the relentless enemy of understanding. (J.K. Galbraith "The Affluent Society).

Computer – Man is still the most extraordinary computer of all. (J.K. Kennedy 21.05.63).

Master – A hungry person desiring nothing but to fill his belly—for him his belly is his God. To him every one who gives his bread is his master.

Child – If a child is turning to a machine for friendship, it means that he or she has lost faith in human relationship.

Sweat – The person who wants to make it has to sweat. There are no short-cuts. And you have got to have the guts to be hated.

Policy – Wherever force has failed, policy often has prevailed. (And policy has no common-sense). (Bismark)

Gossip – In old days people fought with hatchets but now they have burried those and have been fighting with gossip.

Behaviour – Educating managers not only prepares them to know more but also helps for behaving differently.

Penetrate – Try not to stay on the surface of the facts. Do not become only the archivist of facts. Try to penetrate into the secrets of their occurrence, and search out the laws which govern them.

Dark horses – Dark horses often make the shrewdest of winners. Hand picked persons are found good if there is no interest.

References

Bass, Bernard M., Leadership, Psychology and Organisational Behaviour (1960), Harper and Row, USA.

Drucker, Peter F., New Realities (1990) USA Task Responsibilities and Practices (1974), Harper and Row.

Kinhall, G.A., Enough of the Talk, Get on with Action (1993), FRI Dahradoon.

Locke, John, An Essay Concerning Human Understanding (1927), Everyman's Library, London.

Monapper A., Industrial Relations (1988), Tata McGraw Hill, New Delhi.

Odum H.T., Environment, Power and Society (1971) Wiley Interscience, USA.

Preston C, Resources and Man (1969), WH Freeman, USA.

Rao TV Dr. et. al., HR @ Heart of Business (2002) Excel Books, New Delhi.

Rath S.B., Understanding Elements of Competency (1993), Current Labour Reports, Bombay.

Senge Peter, The Fifth Discipline (1990), Double Day, USA.

Toffler Alvin, The Future Shock (1985), Bantam USA, The Adaptive Corporation (1985), McGrawHill, New York.

Toynbee A.J., Change and Habit (1966), Oxford University Press, London.

Verma M.K., Managing More Effectively (1997), Response Books, New Delhi.

Index

F

G

H

I

J

K